T0328976

ACCUMULATION
IN AN AFRICAN PERIPHERY

A THEORETICAL FRAMEWORK

Issa G. Shivji
Mwalimu Nyerere Research Professor of Pan-African
Studies
University of Dar es Salaam

Published by:
Mkuki na Nyota Publishers Ltd
P. O. Box 4246
Dar es Salaam, Tanzania
www.mkukinanyota.com

This and other Mkuki naNyota Publishers' titles are available outside Africa from:
African Books Collective, Oxford, UK
www.africanbookscollective.com

Michigan State University Press
Lansing, Michigan, USA
www.msupress.msu.edu

ISBN 978-9987-08-031-1

Table of Contents

Abbreviations

AFRICOM	U.S. African Command
AGOA	African Growth and Opportunity Act
BBC	British Broadcasting Corporation
BWIs	Bretton Woods Institutions
CIA	Central Intelligence Agency (the USA spy agency)
CIT	Confederation of Industries of Tanzania
EARC	East African Royal Commission
EPA	External Payment Arrears (account)
G8	Group of 8 most industrialised countries
GATT	General Tariffs and Trade
GDP	Gross Domestic Product
Gini	A measure of inequality
HIPC	Highly Indebted Poor Countries
HMO	Health Management Organisation
IFIs	International Financial Institutions
ILO	International Labour Organisation
IMF	International Monetary Fund
IT	Information Technology
ITR	Individualisation, Titling, and Registration
ODA	Overseas Development Aid
PRSP	Poverty Reduction Strategy Paper
REPOA	Research on Poverty Alleviation
SAPs	Structural Adjustment Programmes
SSA	Sub Saharan Africa
TANU	Tanganyika African National Union
UDSM	University of Dar es Salaam
UNCTAD	United Nations Conference on Trade and Development
WTO	World Trade Organisation

Acknowledgements

I am grateful to Research on Poverty Alleviation, Tanzania (REPOA) for supporting the book project of which this monograph is a part. REPOA provides an excellent atmosphere for research and reflection with a very friendly research, library, and support staff. Thanks go also to my friend Professor Sam Moyo of the African Institute of Agrarian Studies for agreeing to publish this as a monograph to contribute to the on-going debate on African development which has assumed dramatic significance with the crisis of the international capitalist system and the beginning of the end of neo-liberalism. I am grateful to Dr. Lisa Maria Noudehou, who edited the manuscript within record time and to Mkuki na Nyota Publishers who agreed to publish it also in record time.

By way of a preface

This monograph is a part of the work-in-progress on the political economy of neo-liberalism in Tanzania. It is adapted from the draft first chapter exploring the current state of African debates on development from the standpoint of political economy. Enmeshed as it is in the worldwide capitalist economy, the Tanzanian political economy cannot be understood outside the global processes of capital accumulation which drive it. The current social and economic debates are very much grounded in monetarist approaches. We thus have had to make a detour in the first section to explain some basic categories of radical political economy, which are the building blocks of our conceptual framework.

With the major crisis facing the developed capitalist economies of North America and Europe, political economy is making a dramatic come-back. Neo-liberal economics based on categories of monetarism is falling woefully short of explaining the multifaceted crises. Political economy, in particular Marxist political economy, provides, at the least, the tools, concepts and categories which can be deployed to make sense of what on the surface appears anarchic. In northern universities there is an increased interest in understanding the methods of historical materialism. In Africa, we are lagging behind. It is time to take a longer view and situate our condition within a bigger picture. The thesis of this monograph is that the best way to understand the big picture is to examine the processes of accumulation. The monograph examines the theoretical framework of the processes of accumulation in an African periphery.

The purpose of the advanced publication of the monograph

is to provoke a discussion on the theories of accumulation. The hope is that a rehabilitation of a political economy discourse will help the younger generation of African scholars to understand better the actual existing conditions of their countries and the continent beyond the monetarist and market categories of neo-liberalism in which they are currently embedded.

Dar es Salaam
January 2009

1

THE DEVELOPMENT DISCOURSE

An Overview

'From development to poverty reduction,' sums up the trajectory of the development discourse in Africa over the last four or so decades since independence. This development marks significant shifts, not only in economic approaches and policies, but also in the academic theories and political ideologies underpinning the discourse. This section briefly reviews the discourse surrounding four aspects: first the institutional and social agency of development; second, its ideological rationalization or justification; third, the theories underlying the discourse, and, fourth, its politics. The contextual theme running through the discourse is Africa's place and role in the global political economy and its relationship with the developed North, or, more correctly, with imperialist forces. The first two decades after independence, roughly the 1960s and 1970s, may be called the 'age of developmentalism'. The next decade, that is the 1980s, has been characterised as Africa's lost decade. This period spawned various structural adjustment programmes or SAPs under the tutelage of the IMF and the World Bank. SAPs prepared the ground for and dovetailed into the next, or the current period, which began in the 1990s, and which may be characterised as the 'age of globalisation'.

The age of developmentalism

The struggle for independence in Africa was primarily an assertion of the humanness of the African people after the five centuries of domination and humiliation through the slave trade and colonialism. In the words of Tom Mboya, the struggle for independence was the 'rediscovery of Africa by Africans' (Mboya 1963: 13), while Amilcar Cabral describes it as the 're-Africanisation of minds' or 're-becoming Africans' (Cabral 1980: xxii, xxv). National development became the passion of politicians and the 'great expectation' of the people. In the vision of the more articulate nationalist leaders, such as Julius Nyerere of Tanzania, the independent state had a double task, that of building the nation and that of developing the economy. The state in Africa, Nyerere argued, preceded the nation, rather than the other way around. Thus, the national project from the start was developmental, top-down, and statist.

The colonial economy and society was anything but national. In the scramble for Africa, the colonial powers had divided the continent into mini-countries where boundaries cut through cultural, ethnic, and economic affinities. The imperial policy of divide and rule made it worse, leaving behind extremely uneven development both within and between countries. Some regions were more developed than others. Some ethnic groups were labelled martial, providing a recruiting ground for soldiers; others were turned into labour reservoirs; some were characterised as intelligent and moderately entrepreneurial, as opposed to the rest, who were characterised as inherently indolent and lazy. All were, of course, denominated as uncivilized, uncultured, undisciplined pagans whose souls needed to be saved and whose bodies needed to be thrashed.

The colonial economy was typically disarticulated, almost tailor-made, for exploitation by colonial capital, linked to the metropolitan trade and capital circuits. Extractive industries like mining predominated. Plantation agriculture existed side by side with subsistence peasant cultivation, both of which concentrated on one or two crops for export according to the needs of the metropolitan economy. In settler colonies, large-scale alienation of fertile land left the indigenous to eke out a living from scraps of land and to pay taxes to the colonial state, all while providing labour to the settler farmer.

Entrepreneurship and skilled labour were deliberately discouraged, if not suppressed, by legal edicts and administrative fiat. Instead, where needed to distribute metropolitan goods, build railways and ports, or service the state and the settler town, such skills were imported from the Indian subcontinent.

Different colonial powers left behind different forms and traditions of public administration, culture, cuisine, dance and education (elementary as it was), all concentrated in towns. The urban and the rural were literally two countries within one: one was alien, modern, a metropolitan transplant barred to the native – while the other was stagnant and frozen in so-called tradition or custom. Neither the modern nor the traditional were organically so. Both were colonial constructs. No other continent suffered as much destruction of its social fabric through foreign imperial domination as did Africa.

I have traced these initial conditions on the eve of independence for two reasons: firstly, to underline the fact that the nationalist project faced a formidable task on the morrow of independence; secondly, to underscore an even more formidable reality, this is that the state that was supposed to carry out the twin task of nation-building and economic development was itself a colonial heritage. The colonial state was a despotic state, a metropolitan police and military outpost, in which powers were concentrated and centralized, where law was an unmediated instrument of force, and where administrative fiat was more a rule, than the rule of law.

The nationalist vision thus called for a revolutionary transformation not only of the economy and society but also of the state. A few nationalist visionaries attempted, but none succeeded. The post-independence international context was no more propitious than the colonial. Independence found Africa in the midst of a cold war and faced with a rising imperial power, the United States of America, for whom any assertion of national self-determination was "communism", to be hounded and destroyed, by force if necessary, by manipulation and deception if possible. Patrice Lumumba, the first prime minister of the Congo, was assassinated, to be replaced by a US stooge, Mobutu Sese Seko, while Kwame Nkrumah was overthrown with the connivance of the CIA. Civil wars fuelled by elite greed and the geo-political interests of imperialist powers tore the continent apart.

These, then, were the initial conditions within which African nationalists had to realise their dream of nation-building and economic development and to answer to the 'great expectations' of their people. Invariably, the agency for change was the state since there was virtually no social class that could shoulder the task of national development. Franz Fanon gave a succinct and graphic account of the African middle class, which inherited power at independence. Fanon said:

> The national middle class which takes over power at the

end of the colonial regime is an underdeveloped middle class. It has practically no economic power, and in any case it is in no way commensurate with the bourgeoisie of the mother country which it hopes to replace. ... The national bourgeoisie of underdeveloped countries is not engaged in production, nor in invention, nor building, nor labour; it is completely canalized into activities of the intermediary type. ... The psychology of the national bourgeoisie is that of the businessman, not that of a captain of industry; and it is only too true that the greed of the settlers and the system of embargoes set up by colonialism has hardly left them any other choice. (Fanon 1963: 119-20)

Nor was foreign capital obliging in spite of various protective laws and incentive schemes put in place by African governments. Invariably, nationalist politicians turned to the state. African governments of all ideological hues – from capitalist Kenyans to socialist Tanzanians to Marxists of various inclinations– all resorted to the State for their economic programmes. Contrary to the current propaganda of the West, which disowns responsibility, it was their institution, the World Bank that designed the post-independence economic programmes. In effect, the programmes involved intensification of the monoculture agriculture for export, establishment of some enclaves of import-substitution industrialization, and throwing the doors open for the multinationals to invest in extractive and resource based industries.

The public sector expanded rapidly and was financed, almost exclusively, by draining surpluses from the peasantry and the under-paid semi-proletariat. State-run and managed marketing boards became the mechanism of siphoning off surpluses out of the agriculture sector. Incidentally, the marketing board, with a monopoly to buy peasant crops sanctioned by law, was the great invention of the British after the Second World War to enable surpluses from the colonies to be accumulated in the metropolis to finance its reconstruction. Thus, the African soldier not only fought in imperialist wars, but the African peasant also financed the reconstruction of the post-war metropolitan economy.

The state had to be staffed. The colonial bureaucracy was almost exclusively White at the top and immigrant in the middle. The education and health infrastructure had to be expanded, both for pragmatic as well as political reasons. Africanisation of the civil service could not be resisted, nor could the basic welfare demands of the population. Provision of basic services by the state also served to legitimise the otherwise authoritarian rule of the political elite. The state bureaucracy grew by leaps and bounds.

Nationalism thus resolved itself into various ideologies of developmentalism. 'We should run while others walk', politicians declared. The academia was dominated from the North. Modernization, based on Parsonian pattern variables and Rostow's 'stages of economic growth', was the theoretical norm. The mainstream argument was that post-independence economies were typically dual economies. There was the traditional sector, which was rural, unproductive, backward, lacking entrepreneurial spirit, and governed by ascription or the 'economy of affection'. Development consisted in modernizing the traditional society, or, as Goran Hyden would have it, capturing the un-captured peasantry (Hyden 1980). Political scientists thus looked for modernizing elites, from modernizing chiefs to modernizing soldiers as political expediency dictated.

The dominance of the modernization paradigm was challenged by young academics coming out of post-independence universities. Where there was relatively a freer space, as in the Tanzania of the 1960s and 1970s, intense debates raged between modernizers and radical nationalists calling themselves African socialists or *Ujamaaists* or Marxists. Taking their cue from Marxism and the Latin American *dependencia* school, African progressives placed the history of the development of underdevelopment and the role of imperialism as the process of worldwide accumulation at the centre of their analysis and understanding. The traditional, they argued, was not quite traditional, nor the modern quite modern; rather both belonged to the system of international capitalism which reproduced development at the centre and underdevelopment at the periphery. Development therefore was not a process of changing 'pattern variables' or looking for modernizing elites, but rather a process of class struggle. Inherited colonial societies called for fundamental transformation or revolution. Controversies raged around issues of imperialism, class, and state; over identifying the forces of the African revolution and the forces of neo-colonial reaction (Tandon ed. 1982).

Meanwhile, the state became both the site of power struggles as well as of accumulation. Radical nationalists, who showed any vision of transforming their societies, were routed through military coups or assassinations. A few who survived compromised themselves and became compradors or tolerated imperial arrogance for pragmatic reasons. Everywhere, politics became authoritarian, whether in the form of one-party states or outright military dictatorships. Liberal constitutional orders imposed by the departing colonial powers did not survive as the underlying logic of the colonial despotic state reasserted itself (Shivji 2003).

The cold war context and the hegemonic imperatives of imperialism expressed themselves in utter intolerance of any radical nationalist or liberal initiatives. National self-determination and democracy were, and continue to be, the anti-thesis of imperialism.

State positions opened up opportunities for seeking political rents. State and bureaucratic bourgeoisies typically exhibited all the vices that Fanon attributed to them. It is a 'little greedy caste, avid and voracious, with the mind of a huckster, only too glad to accept dividends that the former colonial power hands out to it.' It is incapable of 'great ideas or of inventiveness' (ibid. 141), and is 'already senile before it has come to know the petulance, the fearlessness or the will to succeed of youth', (ibid. 123). Conspicuous consumption at home, a little investment in unproductive activities to make quick profits, and a lot of stashing away of funds in foreign bank accounts were, and perhaps still are, the typical characteristics of this class. Thus, very little serious domestic private accumulation took place. The state was the major investor.

During the first one-and-half decades of independence, African economies showed modest growth, modest in comparison to other continents, but impressive given the initial conditions at the time of independence. Investment and savings ranged between 15 to 20 per cent of the GDP (Adesina 2006: 48). Primary and secondary school enrolment was expanded. Tertiary education, which in many countries literally did not exist during colonial times, was introduced. Medical and health statistics also showed improvement. But this growth and development was unsustainable. It was predicated on the reinforcement of colonial foundations (see, generally, ibid.).

Growth in agriculture was based on extensive cultivation rather than a rise in productivity through 'chemicalization', mechanization, and irrigation. Agriculture depended heavily on the export of a few primary commodities traded on a hostile and adverse international market. The growth in the manufacturing industry was heavily of the import-substitution type with little internal linkages and dependent on import of intermediary inputs for the narrow luxury goods market. Investment was largely public while domestic private capital was stashed away in foreign countries. One estimate has it that by 1990, 37 per cent of Africa's wealth had flown outside the continent (Mkandawire & Soludo 1999: 11). To top it all, foreign capital concentrated in extractive industries, which simply haemorrhaged the economy rather than contributing to its development.

During this period, the developmental state also borrowed heavily whether for productive or prestigious projects. Petrodollars accumulated by international banks during the 1973 oil crisis were off-loaded in the form of cheap loans to developing countries. By the end of the 1970s, cheap loans turned into heavy debt burdens. By this time, the limits of the early growth were also reached and the economic shocks of the late seventies plunged African economies into deep crisis. Numbers fell, growth rates became negative, debt repayments became unsustainable, fiscal imbalances went out of control, and so did inflation. Social services declined, infrastructure deteriorated, and, one after another, African governments found themselves at the door of the IMF and the Paris Club pleading for mercy.

The 1980s, described by economists as Africa's 'lost decade', was also the transition decade which marked the beginning of the decline of developmentalism and the rise of neo-liberalism, euphemistically called, globalisation.

The crisis, the lost decade and the spectre of marginalisation

In 1981, the World Bank published its notorious report, *Accelerated Development for Africa: an Agenda for Africa.* It was certainly an agenda for Africa set by the erstwhile Bretton Woods Institutions (BWIs) with the backing of Western countries, but it had little to do with development, accelerated or otherwise. The report and the subsequent SAPs concentrated on stabilization measures: getting rid of budget deficits, bringing down rates of inflation, getting prices right, unleashing the market, and liberalising trade. According to the World Bank, the villain of the declining economic performance in Africa was the state: it was corrupt and dictatorial, it had no capacity to manage the economy and allocate resources rationally, it was bloated with bureaucracy, and nepotism was its mode of operation. The BWIs would not bail out the crisis ridden economies unless the governments adopted structural adjustment programmes to get stabilization fundamentals right.

Balancing budgets involved cutting subsidies to agriculture and reducing allocations to social programmes, including education and health. Unleashing the market meant doing away with protection of infant industries and rolling back the state from economic activity. The results of SAPs were devastating as many studies by researchers have shown. Social indicators such as education, medical care, health, nutrition, rates of literacy, and life expectancy all declined. Deindustrialization set in. Redundancies followed. In short, even some of the modest achievements of the nationalist or developmentalist period were lost or undermined.

As the international situation changed with the collapse of the Soviet Union, Western imperialist powers regained their ideological initiative. The neo-liberal package of marketisation, privatisation, and liberalisation now became the policy for, but not of, the African states. Good performers would be praised and rewarded with more aid while the insubordinate and recalcitrant would be parodied and left to its own wit. While aid had always come with strings, now there was no attempt to disguise it. Political conditions were added to economic conditions. Policy making slipped out of the hands of the African state as Western financed policy consultants in their thousands jetted all over the continent with blue prints of Poverty Reduction Strategies and manuals for good governance on their computers, gobbling up one third of ODA (Adedeji 1993: Introduction, 5). In 1985, to give just one example, foreign experts resident in Equatorial Guinea were paid an amount three times the total government wage bill of the public sector (Mkandawire & Soludo 1999: 137).[1]

National liberation ideologies have been rubbished and national self-determination itself has been declared passé. Africa is told that it has only one choice: to get fully integrated into the globalised world or be marginalised. The spectre of marginalisation is so rampant that even progressive African scholars dare say that 'Africa may be graduating from being the region with "lost development decades" to becoming the world's forgotten continent' (Mkandawire & Soludo 1999: xi).

11

The former US ambassador to Tanzania, speaking to the country's lawmakers, was blatantly clear on what the superpower expected of African states:

> The liberation diplomacy of the past, when alliances with socialist nations were paramount and so-called Third World Solidarity dominated foreign policy, must give way to a more realistic approach to dealing with your true friends – those who are working to lift you into the twenty-first century, where poverty is not acceptable and disease must be conquered. (Press Release, U.S. Embassy in Tanzania, 29 July, 2003.)

In short, there is no national question; either it has been resolved or it has been rendered irrelevant by globalisation. African leaders are left with few options: They are told, 'you are either with globalisation or doomed!' They have fallen in line, one after another, even if it means disowning their own past. Blair's Commission for Africa report, which consisted of prominent Africans, including one president and one prime minister, bemoans the whole of last three decades, which virtually means the whole of the post-independence period, as "lost decades". The primary responsibility is placed on the African state for bad governance and lack of accountability, totally ignoring the role of imperialism in both the exploitation of African resources and the support of non-democratic regimes when it suited their interests. Africans are told they have no capacity to think and African states are told they have no capacity to make correct policies. Blair's Commission for Africa declared with a straight face:

> Africa's history over the last fifty years has been blighted by two areas of weakness. These have been **capacity** – the

ability to design and deliver policies; and **accountability** – how well a state answers to its people. (2005, p.14, emphasis in the original).

Policy-making, an important aspect of sovereignty, has been wrenched out of the hands of the African state. Two African scholars painfully observe:

> A major irony of African development history is that the theories and models employed have largely come from outside the continent. No other region of the world has been so dominated by external ideas and models. ((Mkandawire & Soludo 1999: vii)

That brings us to the age of globalisation or neo-liberalism, wherein development itself has been declared passé.

The age of globalised neo-liberalism

Globalisation expresses itself in Africa as neo-liberalism. These are a set of policies around stabilization of monetary and fiscal fundamentals on the one hand, and marketisation, liberalisation, and privatisation of the economy, on the other. The failures of earlier SAPs and their unrelenting critique by African intellectuals saw some modification of the programmes in the 1990s. Some palliatives in the form of poverty reduction, debt relief, moderately subsidized primary education, and AIDs funds were granted. In its 1989 report, the World Bank broadened its perspective somewhat by talking about the necessity of sustainable development and going beyond "the issues of public finance, monetary policy, prices and markets to address fundamental questions relating to human capacities, institutional, governance, the environment, population growth and distribution, and technology." (Quoted in Mkandawire

& Soludo 1999: 91) This statement was a listing of issues in economic and narrow technocratic terms rather than a conception of development as the transformation of Africa's colonial economies. But, then, a broad holistic development agenda cannot be expected of the World Bank. Even the narrow technocratic view of development was short-lived. In 1994, the Bank reverted to its original preoccupation with stabilization.

In short, the underlying thrust of the neo-liberal and globalised development "discourse", which centres on policy-making, is deeper integration of African economies into the global capital and market circuits without fundamental transformation. It is predicated on private capital as the 'engine of growth', which in Africa translates into foreign private capital. It centres on economic growth without asking whether growth necessarily translates into development. It banishes the issues of equality and equity to the realm of rights, not development. 'Human-centred and people-driven development' which was the kingpin of African alternatives, such as the *Lagos Plan of Action*, are ignored as African people are reduced to 'the chronically poor' who are the subject matter of papers on strategies for poverty reduction rather than the authors and drivers of development. This discourse makes African states into villains and demonizes African bureaucracies as corrupt, incapable, and unable to learn. This view legitimises the position that Africans need globalised foreign advisors and consultants, who are now termed development practitioners, to monitor and oversee them.

In this discourse, the developmental role of the state is declared dead and buried. Instead, it is assigned the role of a "chief" to supervise the globalisation project under the tutelage of imperialism, now called, development partners. The irony of the Blair Commission for Africa was that it was convened, constituted, and chaired by a British Prime Minister, while an

14

African president and a prime minister sat on it as members. This symbolizes the nature of the so-called "new partnership". The message is clear: the African "co-partner" in African development is neither equal nor in the driver's seat.[2]

However, the neo-liberal project in Africa has not been without resistance. As Nyerere observed in his preface to a book by African scholars, significantly sub-titled, 'Beyond Dispossession and Dependence':

> Africa's history is not only one of slavery, exploitation and colonialism, it is also a story of struggle against these evils, and of battles won after many setbacks and much suffering. (Nyerere in Adedeji 1993: xv)

There have been struggles against SAPs and globalisation in the streets and lecture halls of Africa. African scholars have severely critiqued structural adjustment programmes and indicated alternatives. Even African states and bureaucracies have not surrendered without some fight. There have been attempts to provide alternative frameworks, plans, and programmes such as the *Lagos Plan of Action (1980), The African Alternative Framework to Structural Adjustment Programme for Socio-economic Recovery and Transformation (1989),* and the *African Charter for Popular Participation and Development (1990).* These alternative frameworks have underlined the need for a holistic approach to Africa's development; called for a continental programme of regional integration and collective self-reliance; called upon African states not to surrender their developmental role and sovereignty in policy-making; and have attempted to develop a vision of a human-centred and people-driven development for the future of the continent. The erstwhile Bretton Woods Institutions and the so-called "development partners" have invariably dismissed these African initiatives (see, generally, Adesina 2006: Introduction). Wielding the threat of marginalisation and dangling the carrot of aid, the so-called development partners have dogmatically and persistently pushed through their own agendas, which invariably prioritize the geo-political and strategic needs of the global hegemony and the voracious appetites of corporate capital for resources and profits.

Although the "neo-liberal honeymoon" may be approaching an end, it will not just disappear. People have to struggle against it. People do not struggle when there are no credible alternatives on the horizon. Practical politics in Latin America – witness Venezuela and Bolivia – are once again putting alternative developmental discourses on the historical agenda. In Africa, state politics and policies may be lagging behind Latin America, but African intellectuals are once again passionately involved in the continent-wide debates on African development. There is a kind of resurrection of nationalism and Pan-Africanism (Shivji 2005). Some excellent critiques of neo-liberalism have been produced. Studies of neo-liberal development over the last 25 years show that Africa is nowhere on the path of sustainable development. Economic prescriptions revolve within the same paradigms of trade and aid embedded in the structures of extraverted, export–oriented economies. New ideas on the structural transformation of the political economy of Africa are being debated. These are inspired by the paradigm of nationally autonomous, possibly pan-Africanist, accumulation processes rooted in social democracy. Unfortunately, these debates have by-passed the once active intellectual community of Tanzania, which was one of the leading centres of African development debates during the 1960s and 1970s. While Tanzanian intellectual elites are still mesmerized by the 'growth' and 'poverty reduction' discourses of neo-liberal vintage, street politics seem to be moving ahead. The recent grand corruption scandals involving political elites and the pillaging of natural resources by voracious foreign capital cries out for analytical understanding and explanation of the political economy as well as the mooting of credible alternatives. The work-in-progress, of which this monograph is the first chapter, is an attempt to understand the political economy of Tanzania over the last 25 years in the context of the broader development discourses and the imperatives of post-neo-liberalism.

2

THEORIES OF DISARTICULATED ACCUMULATION

The driving forces of capitalism

Capitalism remains the dominant world system. To understand it, we have to begin with the elementary categories of capitalist accumulation as our point of departure. "Accumulate, accumulate! That is Moses and the prophets!" (Marx 1867:558[3]). Accumulation of capital augments growth. This theory is at the heart of the development of the capitalist system. It is the motive force of capitalism. Accumulation assumes the production of surplus product for it is that part of production that is not consumed. "The surplus product is that part of the total output of an economy that is in excess of what is needed for reproducing and replenishing the labor, tools, materials, and other inputs used or used up in production" (Bowles et al 2005:93). If accumulation is the motive force of capitalism, the driving force of the system is the generation of surplus product, or what under capitalism is called surplus value. Neither the process of generating surplus value nor the process of accumulation can function without a force *outside* the process of production and accumulation, which creates the conditions for and maintains, regulates, protects, and justifies the system of generating and accumulating surplus value. That force is the state. The state is the organised force of society, which commands the monopoly of (legitimate) violence. The state is not only the mid-wife, which delivered capitalism to the world and created the original or initial conditions of the system, but continues to play a central and decisive role in its reproduction.

On the surface, however, capitalism does not appear as a system of generating and accumulating surplus value. Rather it appears as a system of buying and selling commodities driven by the forces of the market, or, Adam Smith's "invisible hand". It was for political economy, both classical and particularly Marxist, to reveal the underlying laws of motion in the system. Thus the total product of society that *appears* as a collection of commodities, or, in value terms, the aggregate value of those commodities, embodies in it three components. These are constant capital (c), variable capital (v), and surplus value (s). Constant capital refers to that portion of the total value which is used to replenish the "tools, materials, and other inputs used or used up in production," (Bowles ibid.) while variable capital is that portion which is used to replenish labour. In conventional mainstream economics, these are roughly equivalent to depreciation and wages respectively. Surplus value refers to that portion of value that is extra, not paid for. It is *produced* in the process of production, but is *realised* on the market. Surplus value appears as the incomes of non-producing classes such as profits, rent, interest, etc. Indeed, the generation of surplus value is the driving force of the system and *raison d'être* for producing commodities in the first place.

Mainstream economics deals with appearances, the commodity. Its various categories are rooted in the institution of the circulation of commodities, that is, the market: prices, interest, rate of exchange, supply, demand, etc. These categories do not allow us to go beyond what appears on the surface to the underlying system of production. The latter is the task of

19

political economy. Political economy gives us the 'big picture'. Who produces, who appropriates, and how the surplus product is disposed of are the big questions of political economy. Classical and Marxist political economy went further than simply developing abstract categories – capital, surplus value, accumulation, necessary product etc. Abstraction is a method of scientific analysis which provides a theory with which to understand and explain our concrete reality. It is not a *description* of that reality. The categories or concepts of analysis are abstracted from concrete reality, which is social. Thus what exists in reality is a capitalist, a worker, a landlord, not capital, wages, or rent. It was the genius of Marx and Engels to develop the method of *historical materialism*, which assists us in discovering, understanding, and identifying the movement of social reality embedded in social relations (Marx 1971 [1859]: 20-21).

The concrete form of abstract categories of analysis is expressed in social actors involved in *historically defined social relations*, which determine the nature and character of the economic system and the social formation. The division of the social product between the necessary and surplus product, the means by which the surplus product is appropriated from the producer, the form it takes, and the manner of its disposal determines the essentials of an economic system. How and by who surplus is produced, appropriated and accumulated in historically determined relations define the important characteristics of a social formation. Focusing on the production and accumulation of surplus thus helps us to understand and explain the 'big picture', as well as its tendencies and movement over time. Accumulation is the *sine qua non* of expanded reproduction or economic development. Mainstream economists narrowly call this economic growth.

The rise and fall of development economics

Development economics was born after World War II with the political liberation of colonised countries in the global South. Sometimes it is wrongly linked to the US Marshall Plan for Europe, which was strictly a plan for *reconstruction* rather than *development*. The true home of development economics, which later expanded into development studies, is the Third World. The post-colonial African nationalist leaders, understandably, were pre-occupied with the issue of development. The period of their formal colonial occupation was relatively short, less than a century, but, unlike any other continent, Africa had undergone the devastation of the slave trade for almost four centuries, 1450-1850. It was from the ravages of such encounters with what was to become the developed world that the first generation of African nationalists embarked on the task of nation-building and economic development. The task of economic development was not simply one of increasing the production of material goods, but, as Nyerere put it, one of asserting human dignity and freedom. The first generation of African nationalists were faced with the twin task of nation-building and economic development. There was no social class to undertake that task. Colonial heritage made sure of that the "middle-class" that inherited state power on the morrow of independence was an "underdeveloped middle class" (Baran 1957, Fanon 1963).

Ironically, therefore, the task of nation-building and economic development squarely fell on the state. One, therefore, did not need Keynesian theory of an interventionist state, then popular in the West, to justify or rationalise the developmental state in Africa (Mkandawire 2001).

Poverty, disease, and hunger were defined as national enemies in Tanzania. Human dignity and equality could not be attained without development, that is, without raising the standards of human well-being and welfare. Forty years later Amrtya Sen was to say something similar, for which he was awarded a Nobel prize in economics: "... economic unfreedom, in the form of extreme poverty, can make a person a helpless prey in the violation of other kinds of freedom" (Quoted in Bowles 2005:89.). The pursuit of economic development was the preoccupation of independent African governments and the veritable subject of passionate debates among academics, intellectuals, and policy pundits. While neo-classical economics based on comparative advantage and the efficacy of trade to bring about growth and development still held sway with policy consultants, theories around unbridled 'free markets' did not have the same legitimacy. On the Campus of the University of Dar es Salaam, young academics and intellectuals feverishly argued the *paths* of economic development and nationalist history. The official policy of socialism and self-reliance, articulated by the ruling party, TANU, in the *Arusha Declaration* of 1967, took academic debates a notch higher, beyond nation building to the struggle for socialism. Influenced by the Latin American *dependencia* school and Samir Amin's centre-periphery model (1990a), the method of political economy was at the heart of analysis. Taking their cue from Hegel's "the truth is the whole" student discussions argued against compartmentalisation of knowledge and for interdisciplinary approaches and methods across disciplines. Marxist and neo-Marxist texts were read voraciously. Marx, Engels, Amin, Baran, Sweezy, Fanon, and Nkrumah, among others, were some of the most respected authors of the time.

22

Marx's method of historical materialism occupied a place of pride. Many of these discussions veered towards exposing the drain of economic surplus from the periphery and its accumulation in the centre thus developing the centre while leaving the periphery underdeveloped. It is difficult to gauge the extent to which these academic and intellectual debates affected national policymaking. It is certain though that many of the participants in the debates went on to occupy important political positions and civil service posts in the country. Students from that generation also imbibed a deep understanding of the global political economy while absorbing theoretical and analytical tools and frameworks, all of which allowed them to see capitalism as a worldwide system and capitalist accumulation as an integral global process of exploitation. Whatever the argument and different schools of thought, no one questioned *development* (Saul & Cliffe eds. 1972, Ruhumbika ed. 1974, Tandon ed. 1982, Shivji ed. 1986 (b), Shivji 1993).

The neo-liberal intervention displaced both development economics and methods of political economy in favour of Friedman's monetarism. Neo-liberalism has been dubbed a "counter-revolution" in development economics (Hettne 1990:216). The succinct summary of neo-liberalism is Friedman's own: "To the free man, the country is the collection of individuals which compose it. ... The scope of government must be limited ... to preserve law and order, to enforce private contracts, to foster competitive markets..." (Quoted in ibid: 215). In one stroke, the neo-liberal prescription demolished the idea of a developmental state in the South and a Keynesian interventionist state in the North. An unfettered free market does not exist anywhere; it is the figment of a liberal's imagination.

Behind the invisible hand of the market lies the visible fist of the state. For an invisible hand of the market to exist, one needs to have a blind eye. In Africa, as was the case in Tanzania, the importance of the prescription for state withdrawal lay not so much in unleashing markets, but rather in setting free the forces of untrammelled accumulation by dispossession.

The first experiment with neo-liberalism was in Chile under Pinochet's *junta*, which overthrew a popularly elected socialist president, Salvador Allende, with the support of Chilean business elites backed by the CIA and the US Secretary of State Henry Kissinger. Pinochet's economic programme was crafted and led by economists based at the private Catholic University in Santiago, the so-called 'Chicago boys'.[4] These Chilean economists had been trained with US funds at the University of Chicago as part of the Cold War programme "to counteract left-wing tendencies in Latin America" (Harvey 2005:8). What they did in Chile finds echoes in much of Africa today, including Tanzania.

> Working alongside the IMF, they restructured the economy according to their theories. They reversed the nationalizations and privatized public assets, opened up natural resources (fisheries, timber etc.) to private and unregulated exploitation (in many cases riding roughshod over the claims of indigenous inhabitants), privatized social security, and facilitated foreign direct investment and freer trade. The right of foreign companies to repatriate profits from their Chilean operations was guaranteed. Export-led growth was favoured over import substitution. (Harvey ibid: 8)

Ronald Reagan in the USA (who was inspired by Milton

24

Friedman) and Margaret Thatcher in Britain (who was inspired by Hayek) became the flag-bearers of neo-liberalism (Toussaint 1999:180-83).5 At the Cancun conference in October 1981, which had been called to discuss development problems, "the neoliberal philosophy was translated into 'global Reaganomics', while the Keynesian strategy contained in the Brandt report (which originally was meant to provide a framework for the discussion) was tacitly buried" (Hettne 1990:216). Nyerere had supported the Brandt Commission (1980), of which his finance minister, Amir Jamal, was a member. Nyerere had gone to Cancun still harbouring hope that even if the right-wing Reagan took a stubborn position, some of the social-democratic friends in the North would support the aspirations of the South, embodied in the new international economic order. But the 1981 Cancun was a turning point in North-South relations. It was the beginning of belligerent and undisguised neo-liberalism on world scale. Reflecting on it some years later, Nyerere could not hide his disappointment.

> It was all very revealing… . The other members from the North at Cancun, at least some elements of them, agreed with much of what we had been talking about … We from the South thought that even if we cannot persuade Reagan, the rest of them who agreed with us would go ahead. What was very revealing, and very depressing was that after Regan said 'no' the other leaders from the North said that was the end. (*Third World Network* 2003)

Neo-liberalism, embedded in the so-called Washington consensus, which is renewed every year in the world's most undemocratic forum, the World Economic Forum at Davos, substantially became the policy of both the IMF and the World Bank. The 'consensus' was unrelentingly, and often, coercively rammed down the throats of African governments in the structural adjustment programmes (SAPs). Neo-liberalism was a response to the failure of Keynesianism in the West and the crisis of over-accumulation, as we shall see. What we need to explore is what it meant for accumulation and development in Africa. This question is dealt with in the following sections.

Imperialist Accumulation under Globalised Neo-liberalism

Primitive accumulation

In political economy, Marx said, "primitive accumulation plays…about the same part as original sin in theology" (Marx 1867:667). Primitive accumulation refers to the original process by which the conditions of the process of capitalist accumulation are created. Capitalist production assumes a set of people with capital or money on the one hand, and another set of people who have nothing else by which to subsist and reproduce themselves except their own human energy or muscle power, on the other. Nature did not produce property-less labourers on the one side and owners of property on the other. They had to be created. Producers had to be expropriated from their means of production. This process of separation of producers from their means of production is the historical process of primitive accumulation. In England, the enclosure movement by which peasants were expelled from their lands becoming proletarians was part of the process of primitive accumulation. The expropriation of agricultural producers helped to dissolve feudal relations in which the peasant was tied to land. In itself, it did not create an industrial capitalist; it only created the possibility for money capital to transform itself into industrial capital. The genesis of industrial capital had its own forms of primitive accumulation (ibid.:ch.xxxi). In this transformation, the previous accumulation of values worldwide through the commercial empire played an important role. This included the looting of treasures from the Americas (Galeano 1971) and the looting of people from Africa as slaves to work on the plantations of the Americas. Eric Williams (1964) describes the process and the role of slavery in the development of industrial capitalism in Europe, particularly in England. Marx graphically sums up what he called the "momenta of primitive accumulation".

> The discovery of gold and silver in America, the extirpation, enslavement and entombment in mines of the aboriginal population, the beginning of the conquest and looting of the East Indies, the turning of Africa into a warren for the commercial hunting of black-skins, signalling the rosy dawn of the era of capitalist production. These idyllic proceedings are the chief momenta of primitive accumulation. (Marx ibid: 703).

The processes of historical primitive accumulation have been described for Africa in a number of studies (See, for example, Davidson 1971 [1963] and Rodney 1972.). We need not go into details. Suffice it to say that while Marx graphically described the role of primitive accumulation from the peripheries, including Africa, he did not have a full-blown theory of imperialism. In fact, he saw the march of European capital into these continents, however brutal it was, a means by which the backward forms of production and society would be brought into the age of modern capitalism, and therefore, progressive.[6] It was for Rosa Luxembourg to deploy the concept of primitive accumulation to explain imperialism.

Luxembourg did not specifically set out to develop a theory of imperialism in her *The Accumulation of Capital* (1963, [1913]; See also Luxembourg and Bukharin 1972). Her main concern was to show that the closed, two-class system (capitalists and workers) that Marx assumed for explaining capitalism led to a crisis of oversupply of commodities which could not be sold for lack of effective demand. This meant that capital could not realise surplus value. This led capital to trade with non-capitalist formations and, if the latter were reluctant, to force them to open up. There have been severe theoretical criticisms of Luxembourg's under-consumptionist thesis. It is not necessary for us to go into that. What is important for us here is to underscore her two major propositions: one, that the process of primitive accumulation is not simply historical, but continues contemporaneously with the development of capitalism, specifically in the periphery; and second that the system of capitalism has always been worldwide. "Capital needs the means of production and the labour power of the whole globe for untrammelled accumulation; it cannot manage without the natural resources and the labour power of all territories" (Luxembourg 1963:365). In this regard, she pointed out the *dual* character of capital accumulation.

> One concerns the commodity market and the place where surplus value is produced - the factory, the mine, the agricultural estate. Regarded in this light accumulation is purely economic process, with its most important phase a transaction between the capitalist and the wage labourer .... Here, in form at any rate, peace,

property and equality prevail, and the keen dialectics of scientific analysis were required to reveal how the right of ownership changes in the course of accumulation into appropriation of other people's property, how commodity exchange turns into exploitation, and equality becomes class rule. The other aspect of the accumulation of capital concerns the relations between capitalism and the non-capitalist modes of production which start making their appearance on the international stage. Its predominant methods are colonial policy, an international loan system – a policy of spheres of interest – and war. Force, fraud, oppression, looting are openly displayed without any attempt at concealment, and it requires an effort to discover within this tangle of political violence and contests of power the stern laws of the economic process. (ibid: 452

The two tendencies of capital accumulation, that is, that of accumulating surplus value produced in the process of production (expanded reproduction) by *economic means*, and that of appropriating values from outside the capitalist production process (primitive accumulation) by *extra-economic force* commonly characterise accumulation in the periphery dominated by peasant forms of production, as we shall see. Whereas for Luxembourg the second aspect related only to the relation between the capitalist and non-capitalist modes on the *international stage*, which continues to this day, primitive accumulation continues also *within* many countries of the periphery *internally* as well. Indeed, what partly defines the disarticulated form of accumulation in the latter is the dominance of the second tendency. To explain what he calls accumulation by dispossession under neo-liberalism, David Harvey (2003, 2005) has very perceptively used Rosa Luxembourg's proposition of the continued existence of primitive forms of accumulation. We will discuss this presently, but first let us look at Lenin's theory of imperialism based on over-accumulation.

Industrial and financial over-accumulation

Drawing on Hobson and Hilferding, Lenin was among the first of Marxist writers to develop a theory of capitalist imperialism (1966 [1917]). His argument was that imperialism, which began in the last quarter of the 19th century, grew specifically out of the capitalist system. It was, in other words, a logical working out of the tendencies inherent in capitalism. Marx had shown that with the rising organic composition of capital (that is more constant as compared to variable capital), there was a tendency for the rate of profit to fall. Thus, capitalism finds itself with surplus capital, not an absolute surplus, but surplus at a certain rate of profit. Hence, there is the push to *export* capital to areas where higher rates of profit can be obtained.

Lenin posited five characteristics of imperialism:

1) The rise of monopolies with the concentration of production and capital. So at the base of imperialism lies monopoly capitalism.

2) The merger of bank and industrial capital giving rise to 'finance capital', and on the basis of this finance capital the creation of a financial oligarchy.

3) Export of capital, as opposed to the export of commodities, takes on greater importance.

4) International monopolies combine and divide up the world amongst themselves.

5)   The territorial division of the world by great capitalist powers is completed.

While there have been many writings since and modifications of Lenin's theory, his basic thesis on the tendency for *the concentration, centralisation, and overaccumulation of capital* underlying imperialism remains valid to this day.[7] In fact, in many ways the features he described have intensified since his days. Both export of capital in search of higher profits and export of commodities (markets) for realisation of profits continues. While it is true that there are more capital and commodity flows among developed countries of the centre then between the centre and the periphery, they are of a different kind. Capital flows among the countries of the centre are more integrative – that is the process is one of averaging out of rates of profit – while between the centre and periphery, capital flows are much more in response to higher rates of profit based on higher rates of surplus value (Mandel 1962:454 et. seq). Types of investments also differ. For instance, capital investments in Africa are largely in strategic and extractive sectors to obtain certain raw materials, fuel, minerals, and other resources. (Anyemedu 2006:267)

The monopolisation and concentration of production, capital, and finance is legendry. In 1995, five advanced capitalist countries (the USA, Japan, France, Germany, and the UK) controlled 168 of the 200 biggest corporations, which controlled 85.9 per cent of the overall turnover of the 200 biggest corporations (Toussaint 1999:12). "Of the world's hundred largest economies, fifty are corporations, and the aggregate sales of the world's ten largest corporations in 1991 exceeded the aggregate GNP of the world's hundred smallest countries. General Motors' 1992 sales revenues ($133 billion) roughly equalled the combined GNP of Tanzania,

Ethiopia, Nepal, Bangladesh, Zaire, Uganda, Nigeria, Kenya, and Pakistan" (Korten 1996: 220-21). The rise of finance capital has gone beyond what Lenin could have imagined. This is not simply bank capital, nor a merger of industrial and bank capital. It is capital *sui generis* born of unregulated trade in currency, speculation, debt, hedge funds, derivatives etc., and giving rise to an oligarchy, which is utterly unproductive, personified by people like George Soros. Soros heads the Quantum Fund, which pocketed $1 billion in 1992 by speculating against the British pound. The former Malaysian Prime Minister, Mahatir Mohamed, accused Soros of organising speculative raids on South East Asian currencies leading to the notorious crash of those economies (Toussaint 1999:63). Finance bears no relation to production. Trillions of dollars move from one market to another in split seconds to take advantage of differing interest and foreign exchange rates. To quote one description:

> Most of the $800 billion in currency that is traded … goes for very short-term speculative investments – from a few hours to a few days to a maximum of a few weeks.… That money is mostly involved in nothing more than making money.… It is money enough to purchase outright the nine biggest corporations in Japan – overvalued though they are – including Nippon Telegraph & Telephone, Japan's seven largest banks, and Toyota Motors.… It goes for options trading, stock speculation, and trade in interest rates. It also goes for short-term financial arbitrage transactions where an investor buys a product such as bonds or currencies on one exchange in the hopes of selling it at a profit on another exchange, sometimes simultaneously by using electronics. (Quoted in Korten 1996:189).

Sub-commandant Marcos of the Zapatista movement observed that after the marvel of the neutron bomb, which only destroyed life while leaving buildings intact, capitalist imperialism had created another marvel, the financial bomb (Quoted in Shivji 2002). We saw the explosion of the financial bomb in the Asian crisis of 1997-1998. There is another one that is on-going, and which resulted from the 2008 collapse of the housing-cum-mortgage markets in the USA (See Bello 2008).

As for the colonial division of the world, no doubt the colonial system is formally dismantled, but control of the economies of former colonies by imperial capital continues unabated. Kwame Nkrumah's argument, about political independence and economic dependence, or neo-colonialism, is far truer today then it was then (Nkrumah 1968 [1965]). Yet it is important to go beyond these general formulations to identify more specifically the new features and content of imperial relations between the centre and the periphery, particularly based on the forms and patterns of accumulation. While Lenin described imperialism as the highest stage of capitalism and Nkrumah called neo-colonialism the last stage of imperialism, history has shown that capitalism has gone to an even higher stage and that neo-colonialism has certainly not proved to be the last stage.[8] Whether this is due to the regenerative capacity or vitality of capitalism or the result of its enormous propensity to destroy and rebuild on self-created ruins is a different matter and a point for debate. Prem Shanker Jha seems to argue something in the latter mode (Jha 2006). Over the 700 years of its history, Jha argues, capitalism has gone though three cycles of accumulation. At each cycle of its expansion, capitalism burst open its 'container', causing enormous destruction in the process. Whatever the merits or demerits of Jha's 'container' thesis, destruction and war, as a feature of capitalist expansion and accumulation, is fully borne out by history. We are currently witnessing this phase of destruction in capitalism's history of accumulation called globalisation.

Destruction-creation as a feature of capitalist-imperialism (War is the highest form of destruction and imperialist wars have proved to be monumentally destructive.) can also perhaps be read into David Harvey's thesis of accumulation by dispossession, although he himself does not argue on that score. This point brings us to the useful concept of accumulation by dispossession underlying the neo-liberal phase.

Accumulation by dispossession

Accumulation by dispossession is the term coined by David Harvey (2003) to explain the processes of accumulation during the phase of neo-liberalism. He combines Lenin's thesis of over-accumulation and Luxembourg's proposition on continued processes of primitive accumulation in the encounter between capitalist and non-capitalist modes, to deepen the understanding of the current stage of capitalist imperialism. The argument is that the two forms of capitalist accumulation, that is accumulation through expanded reproduction and accumulation through primitive means, continue to operate throughout the history of capitalist accumulation on a world-scale. He examines how the "'organic relation' between expanded reproduction on the one hand and the often violent processes of dispossession on the other have shaped the historical geography of capitalism." (ibid:141-2).

34

Harvey periodises the rise of 'bourgeois imperialisms' in three stages. The first stage is between 1870 and 1945, during which European countries carved out the globe into their colonies and semi-colonies. This was the first stage of bourgeois rule, rather than the high stage of capitalism. This is the period of *national* imperialisms rationalised and justified by cultural ideologies of racism and national chauvinism. The second stage from 1945 to 1970 is the period of the rise of American imperial hegemony. This is the period of economic growth and consumerism in the advanced capitalist countries, post-war reconstruction of Europe with Germany and Japan making an impressive re-entry in the world economy, and the Cold War in which the USA saw itself as the policeman of the world rolling back communism. The so-called golden age of capitalism was predicated on "the massive creation of effective demand via rising wages for labor in the North, the reconstruction of Europe and Japan, and the import-substituting industrialization in Latin America and other parts of the South" (Bello ibid.) Unlike European imperialism, US imperialism sought to hegemonise itself through the universal ideologies of human rights, freedom, and democracy. But the logic of individual and national equality that underpin these ideologies and the imperialist imperative of domination inevitably clashed. From the supporter of colonial independence, the USA turned into an oppressor of nations. The post-war period of the rise of US hegemony, was also the period of the former colonised countries seeking to develop themselves, thus unleashing the processes of expanded reproduction, more often than not through the agency of the state. Ideologies of self-determination, anti-dependency, national development, and anti-imperialism held sway, all of which the USA characterised as 'communist' and therefore to be suppressed overtly or covertly. In the periphery, state capitalisms of varied kinds were legitimised politically in the ideologies of state nationalism, socialism, and developmentalism. Although these were not a direct challenge to capitalism, they did challenge the liberal notions of private property, private accumulation, and 'free markets', thus invoking the wrath of Western imperialism.

In this period, world economic hegemony was to be sought and established through multilateral agencies – the IMF, World Bank, GATT etc. – based on the gold standard linked to the US dollar in a fixed exchange rate. The US dollar became the international currency of exchange. The effect of the Cold War and military adventures in the Third World from the Korean to the Vietnam wars made the USA what Eisenhower referred to as the military-industrial complex. In effect, the USA became a 'permanent war economy'. The crisis of over-accumulation was temporarily resolved through the manufacture of arms and fighting wars abroad while maintaining high levels of consumerism at home (Magdoff 1969).[9] The apparent solution was short-lived as the rising costs of military adventures and the war in Vietnam caught up, resulting in fiscal crisis in the USA. The response was to print more dollars, resulting in worldwide inflationary pressures. "The consequence ... was an explosion in the quantity of 'fictitious' capital in circulation lacking any prospect of redemption, a wave of bankruptcies (focused initially on assets in the built environment), uncontainable inflationary pressures, and the collapse of the fixed international arrangements that had founded US super-imperialism after the Second World War." (Harvey 2003:61). The stage was set for the entry of neo-liberalism.

The thirty-year period between 1970 and 2000 is, according to Harvey, the period of the hegemony of neo-liberalism where the neo-liberal construct becomes the 'common sense' of economic and social thought. Harvey's succinct description of neo-liberalism should be quoted:

> Neoliberalism is in the first instance a theory of political economic practices that proposes that human well-being can best be advanced by liberating individual entrepreneurial freedoms and skills within an institutional framework characterized by strong private property rights, free markets, and free trade. The role of the state is to create and preserve an institutional framework appropriate to such practices. The state has to guarantee, for example, the quality and integrity of money. It must also set up those military, defence, police, and legal structures and functions required to secure private property rights and to guarantee, by force if need be, the proper functioning of markets. Furthermore, if markets do not exist (in areas such as land, water, education, health care, social security, or environmental pollution) then they must be created, by state action if necessary. But beyond these tasks the state should not venture. State interventions in markets (once created) must be kept to a bare minimum... (Harvey 2005: 2).

Neo-liberalism was at once an economic prescription, as well as an ideological attack on notions of *collective* property (socialism), *national* development (national liberation), and *social* solidarity (trade unionism), which had gained ascendancy during the Cold War (Furedi 1994). The notion of *individualism* was stretched to the extreme, beyond the individualism of enlightened bourgeois liberalism. Thatcher declared there was "no such thing as society, only individual men and women" and (she later added) their families (Quoted ibid: 23).[10] She was responsible for undermining historically created strong working class solidarity in Britain by her vicious attack on the Mining Union. Together with Reagan, she pushed the neo-liberal agenda onto the Third World, including Africa, through the IMF and the World Bank and then the WTO. Force, fraud, deception, carrot, and stick, have all played a major role in the propagation of neo-liberalism in the South, particularly Africa. The installation of the vicious dictator in Chile was the first laboratory where neo-liberalism was tested. Bush and Blair, the notorious successors-in-ideology of Reagan and Thatcher, later applied it in Iraq. The first four decrees of Paul Bremmer, head of the Coalition Provisional Authority in occupied Iraq, promulgated on 19 September 2003, included "the full privatization of public enterprises, full ownership rights by foreign firms of Iraqi businesses, full repatriation of foreign profits...the opening of Iraq's banks to foreign control, national treatment for foreign companies and...the elimination of nearly all trade barriers" (Quoted in Harvey, ibid: 6). These are the very conditionalities that the World Bank and the IMF impose on African countries, including Tanzania; that the USA incorporates in its aid (See AGOA and Millennium Challenge Account); and that Western powers have been aggressively advocating at WTO negotiations.

Heart-stricken by poverty-stricken Africa, Tony Blair took the lead for humanitarian aid to Africa.[11] His hyped-up initiative on "making poverty history" fell flat on the ears of his Davos compatriots. Blair's close associate, a senior British diplomat,

Robert Cooper, provides the philosophy, the theory, and the rationale of Blair's intervention.

> The challenge of the post-modern world is to get used to the idea of double standards. Among ourselves, we operate on the basis of laws and open cooperative security. But when dealing with more old-fashioned kinds of states outside the post-modern continent of Europe, we need to revert to the rougher methods of an earlier era – force, pre-emptive attack, deception, whatever is necessary to deal with those who still live in the nineteenth century world of every state for itself. Among ourselves, we keep the law but when we are operating in the jungle, we must also use the laws of the jungle. In the prolonged period of peace in Europe, there has been a temptation to neglect our defences, both physical and psychological. This represents one of the great dangers of the post-modern state....

> What is needed then is a new kind of imperialism, one acceptable to a world of human rights and cosmopolitan values. We can already discern its outline: an imperialism which, like all imperialism, aims to bring order and organisation but which rests today on the voluntary principle.

> Post-modern imperialism takes two forms. First there is the voluntary imperialism of the global economy. This is operated by an international consortium through international financial institutions such as the IMF and the World Bank – it is characteristic of the new imperialism in that it is multilateral. These institutions provide help to states wishing to find their way back into the global economy and into the virtuous circle of investment and prosperity. In return they make demands

which, they hope address the political and economic failures that have contributed to the original need for assistance. Aid theology today increasingly emphasizes governance. If states wish to benefit, they must open themselves up to the interference of international organizations and foreign states (just as, for different reasons, the post-modern world has also opened itself up. (Cooper 2002).

The broad thrust of globalised neo-liberalism may be summarised in six main characteristics, all of which find local expression, with of course, Tanzanian characteristics. Firstly, the intense and virtually universal push for *commodification and privatisation* of tangible and intangible human wants and needs. No doubt, the basis of the capitalist mode of production is commodity. Witness Marx's opening statement in *Capital*: "The wealth of those societies in which the capitalist mode of production prevails, presents as 'an immense accumulation of commodities,' its unit being a single commodity" (Marx 1867:43).[12] The process of commodification in African societies where the capitalist mode of production does not prevail goes on unabated, albeit in distorted forms. This is the integration of the pre-capitalist modes in the globalised world market which Bello calls "extensive accumulation" (Bello ibid). Superimposed on this process is the process of commodification and re-commodification peculiar to neo-liberalism. Marx had noted the creation of artificial commodities (for example, a painting) while Karl Polyani showed how land, labour, and money, for example, are unnatural commodities (Harvey 2005:166). The creation of artificial and unnatural commodities knows no bounds under neo-liberalism. The environment, ecology, other creations of nature (flora and fauna), bio-resources (plant plasma and human embryos), are all turned into commodities, as are emotional relations and pleasures. Even the bane that pollution is for the people of the earth is turned into a boon for capital as typified by carbon trading (*Development Dialogue* 2006). On real objects and relations are erected virtual objects and relations, which in turn are commoditised; in the realm of relations, note the phenomena of cyber girls, private chat rooms, and virtual lovemaking.

There is also the whole process of re-commodification. This takes two forms. Public goods and services (water, energy, education, communication, health, safety, security, and personal integrity), which were once considered to belong to the public domain, are commoditised and privatised. Denationalisation and privatisation of state assets also involves re-commodification in that the assets are now operated according to the forces of the market, whereas previously other considerations would have intervened, making them less than pure commodities. The high point of the process of commodification and privatisation is the 'contracting out' of war to private corporations as has happened in Iraq. [13]

The second feature of globalised neo-liberalism is the pervasive nature of predatory and speculative financialisation of capitalism. This goes beyond the merger of financial and industrial capital and, on its basis, the rise of a rentier class (the coupon clippers), that Lenin talked about. The most illustrative aspect of this process is speculative trading in stocks and currencies by simply moving around fictitious funds electronically. Trillions of dollars move across national borders and different fiscal regimes in a split second. This is facilitated by deregulation of capital and currency markets, creation of stock exchanges, and computerisation of financial transactions, or, fetishization of IT. The IMF and the World Bank insist on liberalisation of financial markets and creation of stock exchanges even in puny, and substantially subsistence, economies like that of Tanzania. Capital movements in and out of Third World economies which can trigger off a financial crisis, whatever the immediate reasons for it, can cause havoc and devastation in a Third World country while enriching a narrow band of elites in advanced countries. This is exactly what happened in the Asian crisis of 1997-8. The following description of the East Asian crisis by Stiglitz is apposite:

> The IMF first told countries in Asia to open up their markets to hot short-term capital. The countries did it and money flooded in, but just as suddenly flowed out. The IMF then said interest rates should be raised and there should be fiscal contraction, and a deep recession was induced. Asset prices plummeted, the IMF urged affected countries to sell their assets even at bargain basement process... The sales were handled by the same financial institutions that had pulled out their capital, precipitating the crisis. These banks then got large commissions from their work selling the troubled companies or splitting them up, just as they had got large commissions when they had originally guided the money into the countries in the first place. (Stiglitz 2002:129-30)

This back and forth movement of money, in effect, resulted in the devaluation of the national assets in these countries; the end result was that the assets passed into the hands of foreign companies from national companies at fire-sale prices. Moreover, in the process financial institutions (largely foreign banks) made large sums of money in the form of commissions. No new values were created. It was only a *transfer* of values from a periphery to the centre. Therefore, while accumulation of capital took place in the centre, misery, unemployment, and pauperisation accumulated in the periphery. Stiglitz describes this process succinctly:

> As the crisis progressed, unemployment soared, GDP plummeted, banks closed. The unemployment rate was up fourfold in Korea, threefold in Thailand, tenfold in Indonesia. In Indonesia, almost 15 per cent of males working in 1997 had lost their jobs by August 1998, and the economic devastation was even worse in the urban areas of the main island, Java. In South Korea, urban poverty almost tripled, with almost a quarter of the population falling into poverty; in Indonesia, poverty doubled … In 1998, GDP in Indonesia fell by 13.1 per cent, in Korea by 6.7 per cent, and in Thailand by 10.8 per cent. Three years after the crisis, Indonesia's GDP was still 7.5 per cent below that before the crisis, Thailand's 2.3 per cent lower. (Ibid: 8)

Malaysia was one of the few countries where the devastation was not as acute because it had refused to deregulate its capital markets. Ironically, East Asian Tigers were once held up as a success story of IMF's neo-liberal policies, and African leaders were cajoled to learn from them. The truth is that in their growth and developmental period before they opened up, these countries did not follow liberalization prescriptions. Rather they were regulated economies tightly controlled by state bureaucracies (See, for example, Amsden 2001). Their development path essentially involved a highly interventionist developmental

43

state, with myriad controls over, not only markets, but also production. In more than one respect, they resembled centrally planned economies. It is following liberalisation *a* ⊠ IMF that their economies fell prey to 'predatory' capitals resulting in the devastating crash of 1997-8.

Financialisation and commodification have completely unlinked real values from market values. Public debt itself is commoditised. The sovereign debt of an African country is bought at a discount by a commercial company or 'vulture capital'. As the country becomes creditworthy, say, due to cancellation of its debts under HIPC, the commercial company embarks on litigation to recover the full debt with interest from the debtor country. A recent case filed against Zambia illustrates the point. In 1979 Zambia incurred a debt to Romania from whom it purchased agricultural machinery and services. Zambia defaulted and the two countries were on the verge of renegotiations to liquidate the debt when Donegal International, a company registered in the British Virgin Islands and owned by an American businessman, bought off the debt at a heavily discounted price of less then $4 million. This was in 1999. The company then negotiated a settlement with Zambia, when it was under Chiluba, under which Zambia would repay the debt to the value of $15 million. The settlement agreement included severe penalty clauses should Zambia default. Sometime in 2007, the company filed a suit against Zambia in a British court claiming some $55 million. Zambia sought to have the case dismissed on the grounds that the settlement agreement had been obtained by the company paying $2 million as a bribe into President Chiluba's favourite charity in return for a favourable settlement. The company denied the charge, saying that it was 'a charitable donation' to 'a low income housing initiative' in Zambia. On legal grounds, the court did not accept Zambia's argument. The court did not award Donegal what it had claimed, but the amount awarded was almost four times what the company originally paid for the debt. Ironically, the claim by the company, if it had been fully upheld, would have wiped off all the debt relief that Zambia had obtained under HIPC after six years of following gruelling conditions set by the IMF and the World Bank (Tan 2008:20-21).

Militarization is the third significant feature of globalised neo-liberalism. During the Cold War militarization was attributed to and rationalised as a response to the threats posed first by the so-called "iron curtain" (the Soviet Union) and then by the "bamboo curtain", or the "yellow peril" (China). Reagan made no such distinctions. In his 'born-again' Christian mind, they were all simply 'evil empires'. With Gorbachev's 'glasnost' and the collapse and disintegration of the Soviet Union, and with China under Deng Xiaoping taking the neo-liberal path, predictably with Chinese characteristics, there was a big hype among the people of the North that the world was about to reap peace dividends. Little did they realise that while the *peaceful* Cold War reigned in Europe, the peoples of the Third World were subjected to hot, proxy wars. Nonetheless, the bi-polar world allowed at least some nationalist, developmental states space to manoeuvre to defend their interests in such organisations as the non-alignment movement or UNCTAD. The post-Cold War proved to be very different.

Militarization and war are inherent in imperialism. The first Gulf War heralded the beginning of the exclusive military hegemony of US imperialism. Since then, it has been a continuous war, in not only the usual theatre of imperial wars, the Third World, but also in Europe. Chickens came home to roost as mini-wars broke out with the disintegration of the Balkan states. The high point was 9/11, which finally shattered the peaceful bliss of ignorance that the Americans laboured under. Bush took on Reagan's born-again mantle as he declared crusades against 'Muslim fundamentalists'. In the mindset of 'born-agains', Saddam Hussein, who was once a protégé of the USA, became an Al Qaeda operator. The world witnessed one of the most gruesome wars, the Iraq war, which has fundamentally changed the perception of the USA in the eyes of the world's people. The thin veneer of the image of champion of democracy, freedom, and human rights that covered the imperial role of the USA has evaporated. Public opinion regarding President George Bush plummeted all over the world. When he left office in 2008-9, he was perhaps the most unpopular US president. The US economy is witnessing one of the worse economic crises ever. Its neo-liberal hegemony, the so-called 'Washington Consensus', is collapsing in its own backyard, Latin America. While Chavez of Venezuela and Morales of Bolivia oppose the USA directly, even 'friends' like Brazil and Argentina are demanding to be treated with deference.

China, and to some extent Europe, is severely competing with the USA in search for energy and other natural resources (See, generally, Khanna 2008). And China is doing it pretty well. In this renewed wave of primitive accumulation on the terrain of natural resources, both, the declining hegemonic power (USA), and the rising one (China) are turning to the African continent. China deploys its economic muscle, while the USA is grinding its military teeth, for military superiority is all that it has left. The documents and plans produced by a clique of neo-conservatives, including Wolfowitz, Cheney, and Rumsfeld in the early 1990s even before 9/11, focussed on establishing absolute military global power. One observer who has studied these documents summarises the plan as follows:

> The Plan is for the United States to rule the world. The overt theme is unilateralism, but it is ultimately a story of domination. It calls for the United States to maintain its overwhelming military superiority and prevent new rivals from rising up to challenge it on the world stage. It calls for the dominion over friends and enemies alike. It says not that the United States must be more powerful, or most powerful, but that it must be absolutely powerful. (Quoted in Harvey 2005 [2003]: 80)

Multiple conflicts in Africa, of whatever immediate origin, provide fertile ground for the US military to penetrate, here under the guise of humanitarianism, there under the pretext of rescue operation, and somewhere else under HIV/AIDs programmes.[14] The USA (followed by Britain) is one of the biggest arms sellers to Africa. Commercial sales of weapons and equipment by the USA to sub-Saharan Africa under the State Department's oversight in 2000 were worth $900,000. In eight years it had rocketed by over 10 times to $92 million. Just in two years, between 2006 and FY 2008, it rose by 80 per cent (LeMelle 2008: 2). The creation of a centralised Africa Command (AFRICOM) within the US army is the latest military thrust into Africa. The original proposal for AFRICOM came from James Jay Carafano and Nile Gardiner of the Heritage Foundation, a neo-con think tank. In a Policy Brief for FPIF, Gerald LeMelle summarises the proposal:

The Carafano/Gardiner proposal makes clear that the objective is to preserve U.S. access to African oil and other natural resources on the continent. Africa produces 90% of the world's cobalt; 64% of its manganese; 50% of gold; 40% of platinum; 30% of uranium; 20% of total petroleum; 70% of cocoa; 60% of coffee; over 80% of coltan and 50% of palm oil. The Heritage report also points to the strategic importance of Africa in the global "war on terror". (ibid: 2)

Militarization of aid to Africa is becoming a reality each day. The militarised face of globalised neo-liberalism is knocking at the door even before Africans have fully recovered from SAPs.

Polarisation is the fourth feature of neo-liberalism. Inequality is inherent in capitalism, but under neo-liberalism it takes extreme forms, both between the countries of the North and the South and within the countries. The richest 1% of people (50 million households) earn more than the 60% of households (2.7 billion people) at the bottom of the income distribution (BBC 2001, see also Milanovic 2007). In the 1990s, one United Nations study reported that 225 rich people in the world had a combined wealth of more than $1 trillion, which was equal to the income of 47 per cent of the world's population, or 2.5 billion people. The three richest men on the planet had assets that exceeded the GDP of 48 of the least developed countries (Quoted in Peacock 2002:7). A study in 2005 showed that in 2002, the Gini for inter-country inequality was 58 points, while the global inequality for households was 70 points. Between 1988 and 2002, the latter Gini increased by 7 points.

Over the 30 years of neo-liberalism in the USA and the UK, inequalities between the rich and the poor have increased enormously. The richest 10 per cent of Americans own 70 per cent of assets, while the bottom 50 per cent own only 2.5 per cent of the assets. Between 1966 and 2001, median wage in the USA remained almost the same while the income of the top 10 per cent increased by 58 per cent. Even more striking in both countries has been that within the rich category, the super rich have become even richer. The income of the top 1 per cent increased by 121 per cent, that of the top 0.1 per cent by 256 per cent while the income of the richest 0.01 per cent increased by staggering 617 per cent (Irvin 2007:6-7). Much the same picture emerges for the UK.

The phenomenon of the super rich getting richer within the generally rich, both at the international and country level, has had another impact. A reasonably prosperous 'middle-class' composed of a significant proportion of the population, which was supposed to demonstrate the 'human face' of capitalism, has virtually disappeared under neo-liberalism. With the collapse of the 'socialist bloc, the 'middle-class' at the level of countries, the second world, has gone off the map. At a social level the so-called middle class at the global level has become more of a group of hirelings for the super rich elites, rather than a middle-class (Peacock 2002:9-10). In any case, its fate is doomed. As one author puts it:

> [T]he interests of the 'middle classes' are always represented in bourgeois society as being those of the political 'middle ground' which is supposed to constitute the majority of the population. ...

> The size of today's middle classes is dramatically down on the 20 per cent of the population that was the usual national average half a century ago. Each major

economic crisis reduces their numbers still further ..... .
(Peacock 2002:22)

In the USA, the middle class is estimated to be only 3 per cent. In other developed countries its numbers are diminishing (ibid.). Irvin describes the fate of the middle class thus:

> As the rich fight to become very rich, the middle class finds its footing on the ladder ever more precarious, skilled public service workers cannot find houses near their jobs, semi-skilled find can't make ends meet and a new 'permanent' underclass emerges which can no longer aspire to getting near the base of the ladder of opportunity, still less to climbing its lower rungs. (Irvin 2007:21)

The fate of the middle class in a periphery is no different although not quite the replica. A genuine middle-class grounded in production and involved in the chain of accumulation is constantly stifled. In the last 15 or so years in Tanzania, for example, we have seen extreme polarization between the "super rich" (by Tanzanian standards) neo-liberal elites on the one hand and the extreme poor majority on the other. What appears as a middle-class is mostly involved in services and business, hardly in production. Firstly, it is minuscule in number. Secondly, its existence is fragile and precarious. Thirdly, it is servile and constantly under the threat of being pushed down. Sometimes the *wamachinga* (street hawkers) and *mama ntilies* (women food sellers) are described as *wajiriamali* (entrepreneurs). These are not entrepreneurs or middle class in any sense of the word, but rather semi-proletarians, who could more appropriately be described as an 'underclass' rather than a middle class. A genuine middle class in an agricultural country like Tanzania would be a rich peasantry constituting a significant proportion of the population. But as various studies have shown, such a middle class is either stifled or merchantilised through perverse processes of accumulation in the context of a peripheral economy (See Gibbon 1995).

The *ephemerality* of relations and *shortening of time horizons* is another feature, which expresses itself in dramatic fashion under neo-liberalism. There is no permanency of job and social security. Labour is fragmented. Short-term, part-time, and casual labour is preferred. This is the so-called labour *flexibity*, which guides the neo-liberal labour regimes in Africa.[15] Tri-partite negotiations on terms and conditions of work, which was the hallmark of bourgeois liberalism and embedded in ILO Conventions, is replaced by bi-partisan decision-making between the state and capital. In Africa, more often than not, it is actually unilateral as capital wields the stick of withdrawing investment should the government fail to oblige.[16]

Social security is marketised; it is neither the responsibility of the employer nor the state. Instead, insurance multinationals offer, and HMOs manage, 'social protection' as so many varied products, all out to make profit from the sick, the old, and the unemployed. The effect is to commoditise *social wage goods*, reclaim it for capital, and make further profit. It thus depresses necessary consumption. In effect, it is a form of primitive accumulation or accumulation by dispossession in that profit or surplus value cuts into necessary product.

Short time horizons inform investment decisions. Money is to be made quickly and one way of doing it is by trading in money rather than in commodities. Production of commodities involves long gestation periods. New forms of predatory capital have no time for that. They either capture already existing values by whatever means they can, or pillage natural resources or quickly turn them into commodities. "Speculative finance", Bello says, "boiled down to an effort to squeeze more 'value' out of already created value instead of creating new value." (Bello ibid). Public debt itself is commoditised and traded at a discount, creating conditions for con men (or *mafisadi* as we call them in Tanzania) to siphon off millions of dollars from the public treasury.[17]

Ephemerality pervades even social relations and production of knowledge. Summer flings replace lasting love and the post-modernist's agnosticism and cynicism regarding human values and decency crowds out knowledge and ethics. The fleeting cartoon images, none of which lasts more than a few seconds, become the daily TV diet for children. Teachers and university professors constantly complain of the lack of concentration and focus in their students. Essay writing is replaced by multiple-choice questions, while sustained research is mutilated at the hands of rapid appraisals. Opinion polls are presented as *voices of the people* while *people's votes* are stolen, crudely in "young democracies" and sophisticatedly in "mature democracies". Our erstwhile consultant-analysts attribute rigged elections in an African periphery to cultural-deficit or tribal proclivities of Africans, while machine-stolen votes in Florida or Ohio go unnoticed. Instead, the verdict of an unelected body, the court, is hailed as the triumph of democratic institutions. At worst, the blame is laid on a neo-con Bush and his cronies, not on Texans or Americans, and much less, on the undemocratic proclivities of the oil oligarchy. Umpteen tabulations of "yes, no, don't know" answers go under the name of *analysis*. Theory is eschewed; struggle is demonised. Instead, unguided short-term fixes are elevated to solutions for human predicaments and poverty.[18] Abstraction, a scientific method of building theoretical knowledge, mega-narratives, whether in social sciences or the arts, historical analysis of global processes and social tendencies are all considered *passé*. Instead, academics gravitate to consultancies and advertise themselves as policy analysts churning out reams, or rather flash-disks, of cut-and-paste reports, which repeat the same things over and over again in different styles and colours of power-point presentations.

True, the trends described here apply only to very few elites in Africa, (and that too in a caricatured form), whereas the large majority of the people are too burdened with basic survival to be thus enamoured. Nonetheless, people are neither marginal nor unaffected, because it is the poor majority that ultimately bear the burden of their elite's frivolities and vulgarities.

While the processes of commodification, privatisation, and militarization described above have been worldwide, including the countries of advanced capitalism, their effect in Africa has been devastating. In the language of accumulation, we could sum up by saying that the destruction of accumulation by dispossession is imposed on African societies without having enjoyed the historical fruits created by the development of accumulation by expanded reproduction. In this sense, imperialism in its neo-liberal phase continues to be a plunderer, rather than 'the pioneer of capitalism', as Warren claimed it to be (Warren 1982). Paul Baran's graphic description of the effects of the encounter between the peoples of the underdeveloped countries and Western capitalism penned half a century ago could well be repeated, with necessary changes, for today's Africa under globalization:

> Thus the peoples who came into the orbit of Western capitalist expansion found themselves in the twilight of feudalism and capitalism enduring the worst features

of both worlds, and the entire impact of imperialist subjugation to boot. ... . Their exploitation was multiplied, yet its fruits were not to increase their productive wealth; these went abroad or served to support a parasitic bourgeoisie at home. They lived in abysmal misery, yet they had no prospect of a better tomorrow. They existed under capitalism, yet there was no accumulation of capital. They lost their time-honoured means of livelihood, their arts and crafts, yet there was no modern industry to provide new ones in their place. They were thrust into extensive contact with the advanced science of the West, yet remained in a state of the darkest backwardness. (Baran 1957: 144)

Thus, the character of exploitation (that is surplus extraction) and accumulation (that is surplus disposal) assumes a 'distorted', or, a disarticulated form in the African periphery leading to its *underdevelopment*. To this subject, we turn next.

3

ACCUMULATION IN AN AFRICAN PERIPHERY

The perverted logic

Both the capitalist logic of exploitation and accumulation and the territorial logic of state administration and jurisdiction were introduced to Africa by capitalist imperialism. The early encounter of Africa with Europe was not *commercial*, involving a mutual exchange of commodities, but rather the *unilateral looting* of human resource. African slavery was neither a trade, nor a mode of production. It was simply a robbery of a people on a continental scale perpetrated over four centuries through force of arms. In the Americas, too, there was massive looting of resources by the Europeans, but there it was looting of gold and copper and other treasures while the human being was simply destroyed, or driven into zoos called reserves, to make way for European settlement (Galeano 1971). On the treasures looted from indigenous people and on their death and destruction, and with the emulation of science and technology developed in their 'motherland' Europe, the capitalism of the 'new world' was built, to which African slave labour made a huge, albeit forced, contribution. The history of plunder and looting in the encounter between Africa and Europe has continued to bedevil the relationship between the Northern centre and the African periphery.

The colonial encounter, which introduced the capitalist economic logic and the territorial state logic, is of a much shorter period seen from the vantage point of history. In Asia, for example, where the European commercial empire did loot and distort the internal logic of development, it did not manage to destroy it, thus leaving the possibility of the re-emergence of the internal logic, even though the colonial encounter there was much longer than in Africa.

The logic of primitive accumulation is plunder, meaning expropriation of values without exchange. The logic underlying capitalist accumulation is exchange of equivalent values, at least in form. Primitive accumulation in Marx's schema therefore was a *prior condition* to enable the functioning of capitalist logic. In the periphery, even in the historic stage before neo-liberalism, primitive accumulation was not completed in the sense of fully separating the producer from his means of production, land. As a prior condition of capitalism, primitive accumulation is distorted, such that it is constantly reproduced. In that respect, accumulation by dispossession in Harvey's sense has always existed in the periphery, taking different forms in different historical periods. Yet, to the extent that capitalism introduces commodity exchange, and production of values in the periphery is integrated in the global commodity circuits, however partially, the capitalist logic of accumulation by expanded reproduction also operates as a tendency. The relationship between the two tendencies, that is, accumulation by dispossession and accumulation by expanded reproduction, and the territorial terrain (national or international) on which they operate, determines the character of accumulation in the periphery. In investigating the political economy of accumulation in the periphery, therefore, one must identify the two tendencies, their relationship and their specific forms as well as the terrain of their operation and the contradictions thus generated. The contradiction between the capitalist and the territorial logic presents itself in the periphery as the contradiction between accumulation by dispossession and accumulation by expanded reproduction on the one hand (capitalist logic), and the contradiction between nation and imperialism (territorial logic), on the other. These contradictions underpin the developmental debates of the post-independence period to which we now turn.

The developmental debates

The developmental debates, whether from the Right or the Left, were evidently structured on the understanding of capitalist development in the centers of capitalism in the West. Development meant *capitalist* development along the path supposedly traversed by the West. The difference between the mainstream economists and radical political economists lay in their understanding of the nature of the contact between the capitalist West and the undeveloped South and its effect on the latter. Stages-of-growth theorists such as Rostow saw underdeveloped societies at some stage on the linear path of development that Western countries had supposedly traversed. Their analysis revolved around identifying forces, which would pull them along this developmental path, and obstacles and constraints that impeded the journey. Typically, in the typologies of mainstream economists, the forces that would pull the undeveloped countries out of their underdevelopment were *external* (foreign capital, technology, Weberian rationality, education, expertise, Western educated elites, or the modernizers, as Iliffe (1973) called them) while the obstacles to development were *internal* (traditions, ignorance, peasant irrationalities, 'economies of affection', as Goran Hyden (1980) characterized it). Among Marxists and neo-Marxists, too, (including Marx himself) there were those who believed that, in its expansionist drive, capital would tear down traditional barriers in the periphery and bring about progressive development in the image of Western societies (Warren 1982). On the other hand, the thrust of the *dependencia* school of Latin America and African political economists such as Samir Amin and historians such as Walter Rodney, was to understand the development of capitalism as a worldwide phenomenon into which the peoples of the South had been drawn. For the 'development-of-underdevelopment' school, the process of the development of the centre and the underdevelopment of the periphery was linked organically. The laws of motion of the worldwide system produced development at the centre and underdevelopment at the periphery. The periphery was the site of generating surplus; the centre the site of its accumulation. Their theories revolved around the law of unequal development which was characteristic of capitalism; but in its imperialist stage, it assumed a specific form whereby development in the periphery was blocked, or distorted, or perverted (Rweyemamu 1973, 1980). Accumulation was *disarticulated*, thus incapable of bringing about sustained, self-generating development which would lift the majority of the people out of their backwardness. Beyond this, Marxists and neo-Marxists differed among themselves in identifying the causes, that is, whether the causes were internal or external, whether they were structural or social, or both, and, more

58

importantly, what would be an alternative path, and forces of "autocentric" development (to use Amin's phrase 1990: passim). It is not necessary for us to review these debates, nor to come to a definite resolution of differences at a general abstract level. These are matters of concrete analysis of concrete conditions, and answers could well differ across countries and historical periods. Suffice it to identify some of the important theoretical insights on disarticulated accumulation generated by the debates and relevant for articulating a framework of analysis.

Conceptual framework of disarticulated accumulation

Structural disarticulation:

The point of departure invariably is the colonial, extraverted, vertically integrated economy dependent on primary commodities, both agricultural and mineral. One of the important characteristics of this type of economy is that it answers to the accumulation crises and needs of the centre, thus introducing a series of distortions and disarticulation in the economy of the periphery.

First, there is disarticulation between the structure of production and the structure of consumption. What is produced is not consumed and what is consumed is not produced. Africa continues to export a large proportion of its coffee, cocoa, cotton, tea, palm oil, and gold, diamonds, copper, iron, etc., very few of these products have internal markets. Meanwhile, the import structure is typically characterized by consumer, intermediate, and capital goods in the same order of proportion. The majority of imported consumer goods, moreover, is for the narrow urban and elite markets catering for their internationalized consumption patterns. The needs, particularly for food, of the large majority are catered for by subsistence production or food aid. There are competing demands on peasant labour between producing cash crops for export and food crops for subsistence. It is food production which gives way as less effort is spent on food, leading to food insufficiency both in quantity and nutrition. Food deficiency is typically addressed by either food dumping from the North (destroying home markets) or food aid, thus further reinforcing the dependency syndrome and the disarticulation between food crops and export crops.

The development of agro-fuels, supported by the USA and Europe, is witnessing multinational agribusiness in a new scramble for land in Africa (*Third World Resurgence* 2007). Ironically, the victim of this scramble will be the peasant and the pastoralist as their *minifundia* are turned into *latifundia*, cultivating sugarcane, maize, cassava, palm oil, etc. This is likely to lead to another round of massive primitive accumulation, displacing producers from their lands, destroying forests and ecology, introducing genetically modified crops with far-reaching implication on food chains, and, generally, further integrating the African periphery into "the Atlantic agro-industrial complex" (Moyo and Yeros 2007(a):16). Disarticulation between structures of production and structures of consumption will further deepen, this time around the very basic human need, food.

Second, there is disarticulation between agriculture and industry. There are no, or very few, forward and backward links between these two main sectors. Industries exist as enclaves bearing little relation to agriculture, while both are integrated in the global circuits. Import-substitution industrialization of the post-independence period was characterized by heavy dependence on imports for raw material, machinery, and intermediate inputs, while its products, mainly consumer and intermediate products, catered for narrow urban and elite markets. In absolute terms, Africa's contribution to manufacturing has been low and sub-Saharan Africa's much lower. The spurt of import-substitution industrialization between the late 1950s and 1960s was itself distorted and biased. It was biased against producer and capital goods in favour of consumer and intermediate goods; it was biased against mass consumer goods in favour of narrow elite consumption goods; it was biased against labour-intensive techniques in favour of capital-intensive techniques thus generating very little employment compared with value added. Rweyemamu described this pattern of industrialization as perverse (1973) and argued that this type of "dependency industrialization ... does not enable an economy to generate self-sustaining development and to create an economic system that displays a reasonable symmetry between the structure of production and the structure of consumption." (1980: 2). With the crisis of the late seventies and early eighties and the imposition of SAPs, even this type of industrialization faced a crisis resulting in a spate of deindustrialization in much of Africa. The growth rate of value added in manufacturing industries fell from 3.7 per cent in the first half of the 1980s to a little more than 1 per cent in the early 1990s (Sangare 2006:140). Together with the national project, the industrial project of the post-independence regimes was virtually given up.

Agro-industries involved in processing of agricultural products have remained minimal and elementary with very little value added. In any case, even this processing takes place mainly for export rather than for the domestic markets. With neo-liberalism, and the influx of supermarkets importing processed foods and other agricultural products, agro-processing, however rudimentary it has been, faces extinction.

Lack of industrialization and its organic link with agriculture has persistently reproduced the backward nature of the agrarian sector in Africa. While the conditions for an agrarian revolution (for example, land reform) are created within agriculture, Marx and Kautsky argued long ago that agriculture on its own cannot advance to the next stage of its transformation without machinery, that is, without a simultaneous industrial revolution (Shivji 1987: Amin 1990: 1 et. seq). "Modern industry alone, and finally, supplies, in machinery, the lasting basis of capitalistic agriculture, expropriates radically the enormous majority of the agriculture population, and completes the separation between agriculture and rural domestic industry…" (Marx 700). Colonial capital fares even worse because it destroys rural domestic industry (Kjekshus 1977) and turns the agricultural producer into a pure peasant. The disarticulation between industry and agriculture and the backward nature of agriculture lie at the root of disarticulated structures of peripheral capitalism.

Third, there is intra-sectoral disarticulation in industry as well as between productive sectors and other supportive sectors such as infrastructure, energy, and water. Choice of industries and their geographical location are not integrated with other linked industries or sources of inputs. Typically, industrial plants are put up as turnkey projects, which bear little relation to the overall development of the industrial sector.[19] Samir Amin has summed up structural disarticulation by schematically proposing a four sector model: 1) production of the means of production; 2) production of the goods for mass consumption; 3) luxury production and consumption; 4) exports. In the autocentric or articulated model, sectors 1 and 2 are linked while the disarticulated model is characterized by interrelations between sectors 3 and 4. "This analysis leads to a major conclusion: in the autocentred model labour remuneration (wages and peasants' incomes) must necessarily increase according to the pace of the progress of productivity; in the extraverted model the labour remuneration can be delinked from the productivity growth" (Amin 1990: 7-8).

Exploitation and transfer of surplus:

Contrary to the dominant celebration of flow of resources to Africa in the form of aid and investment, radical political economists have showed repeatedly that the flow of resources is in the opposite direction. Surplus produced in the African periphery is extracted and siphoned off to the centre through various mechanisms. Unfavourable terms of trade between the commodities traded by Africa and the products imported are legendary. Between 1986 and 1990 alone Africa lost $50 billion in export earnings because of declining prices although there was an increase in the volume of its exports by 7.5 per cent. Taking 1980 (=100), the average terms of trade for 1981-1985 were 75.5 per cent, which declined further to only 53.7 during 1986-1990 (Rasheed 1993:50). According to UNCTAD: "Between 1970 and 1997, cumulative terms of trade losses for non-oil exporting countries in SSA amounted to 119 per cent of the regional GDP in 1997 and 51 and 68 per cent of the cumulative net resource flows and net resource transfers to the region, respectively" (Quoted in Adesina 2006). UNCTAD has computed that had it not been for the losses incurred through terms of trade, the per capita income of SSA countries would have been 50 per cent higher in 1997 (ibid. 49).

Debt servicing is another means by which Africa continues to pay tribute to its erstwhile overlords in the North. Between 1982 and 1991, for ten years, sub-Saharan Africa paid $1 billion every month in debt service (Rasheed ibid:60) In spite of this transfer, by the end of 1990s, SSA's debt stock had more than doubled (ibid:61). International debt as a means of exacting usurious tribute was noted by Marx as one of the means of primitive accumulation (Marx 1887: 707). It continues to this day and has become a powerful lever used by imperial centres to not only exact tribute from the periphery, but also to function as a stick to ram policies down the throats of African leaders. Debt relief plans are used to achieve a two-fold purpose: to maintain the integrity of imperial financial systems so that they do not collapse due to un-payable debts, while at the same time, unilaterally, to lay down conditions to keep the debtor countries within the global economic and political orbit. The example of Nigeria is typical. Over a period of 18 years, Nigeria had taken loans worth US$13.5 billion. During the same period it had paid back US$42 billion, almost four times the original loans, while still owing US$36 billion.

> In the preliminary debt negotiations with the Paris Club of creditor countries, in June 2005, Nigeria was required to make an upfront payment of US$12 billion

in order to qualify for an US$18 billion debt write-off. In the period 2000 to 2004, annual external debt service payment averaged US$1.7 billion; the 'debt-write off deal' amounted to collecting in one year what might have taken a little over 7 years to collect! After making the upfront payment, the country's outstanding debt stock would be US$18 billion. Measured against the federal expenditure for 2004, the upfront payment that the Paris Club was demanding would be the equivalent of nearly 10 years' spending on 'social and community services' – education health, etcetera. (Adesina 2006: 24)

According to one UNCTAD study, Africa received US$540 billions in loans between 1970 and 2002 and paid back US$550. Yet in 2002 the continent still owed US$295 billion because of imposed arrears, penalties, and interest (Loong 2007).

Various debt-relief programmes, including HIPC, framed by do-gooders and 'make-poverty-history' advocates are no different. At the end of the G8 conference in 2005, the debt relief was far less than what had been promised. Instead of 100 per cent cancellation of the debt of all poor sub-Saharan African countries, cancellation applied only to 14 SSA countries and it covered debt to multilateral institutions only, not bilateral debt owed to governments. The deal came with strings attached. Gordon Brown, then Britain's Chancellor, underscored that the beneficiaries must maintain their neo-liberal reforms to "boost private sector development and...the elimination of impediments to private investment, both domestic and foreign" (Quoted in Adesina 2005: 23).

Profit repatriation and various other direct and indirect means (manipulation of transfer prices, for example) are used by multinational companies to extract resource flows from the African periphery. All said and done, Africa is a net exporter of resources to the centre rather than the other way round. According to one UNCTAD estimate, in every US$1 of net capital inflow, there is an outflow of 106 cents, 51 cents of which is in terms of trade losses, 30 cents in capital outflow and reserve build-up, and 25 cents in net interest payment and profit remittances (ibid. 49).

Ultimately, it is the peasant and semi-proletarian labour that bears the brunt of exploitation of surplus. The incomplete expropriation of the peasant producer from his/her land in the system of infamous migrant labour was a means by which the peasant family subsidized capital during the colonial period. Mining, road-building, plantations, and settler farms employed men and youth, paying them bachelor wages since the burden of reproduction of labour power fell on the peasant women left behind (Shivji 1986 (a)). Thus labour power was never paid commensurate with its value. It was consistently undervalued. To be able to keep body and soul together, peasant labour exploited itself by reducing its necessary consumption. A combination of monopoly ownership and/or control of land through the state, control over the market, and deployment of extra-economic coercion, enabled the colonial state to maintain and reproduce a system of super-exploitation. Behind the process of what appeared on the surface as commodity exchange, there lay the process of primitive accumulation or accumulation by dispossession. In this case, dispossessing the producers of the capacity to reproduce themselves.

In the post-independence and then neo-liberal period, the process of labour subsidizing capital continues in different forms. The peasant sector is the reservoir of cheap, seasonal, casual, forced, and child labour under various disguises. Unable to survive on the land peasants seek other casual activities – petty trading, craft-making, construction, quarrying, gold-scrapping etc. Foreign researchers document and celebrate these 'multi-occupations' as diversification of incomes and the 'end of peasantry'. It is nothing of the sort. These are survival strategies, which at the end of the day mean that peasant labour super-exploits itself by intensifying labour in multiple occupations and cutting down on necessary consumption (Moyo and Yeros 2007(a):84). Directly, or ultimately, the beneficiary is the dominant capital. The so-called informal sector, for example, providing meagre and fragile livelihoods to thousands of people in any African city, is a kind of subsidy to capital. By over-exploiting itself, the so-called self-employed labour in the informal sector produces cheap wage goods thereby enabling proletarian labour in factories and farms, in turn, to provide cheap labour. Cheap labour and cheap food are the twin pillars on which stands the system of super-exploitation yielding super profits. Hundreds of rural youth migrating to the streets of African cities, the *wamachinga*[20] as they are called in Tanzania, are in effect subsidizing the costs of circulation of commodities, thereby enhancing the profits of merchant capital. The phenomenon of labour subsidizing capital, as opposed to the capitalist logic of labour-power exchanging at value underlying expanded reproduction, lies at the heart of the disarticulated process of accumulation, or accumulation by dispossession. Devaluation of peripheral labour and resources is the lynchpin in the exploitation and transfer of surplus from the periphery to the centre. To understand further we must examine the character of international and local capitals.

Foreign and domestic capitals:

Concentration and centralization of capital giving rise to monopoly capital is the central tendency of capitalism under imperialism. This is not to say that monopoly capital does away totally with competition. Competition between different capitals does exist, but it is characterized by 'unity and struggle'. Cartelization and syndication among big capital is one form of unity. Mergers and acquisitions is a form of struggle resulting in the defeat of some and victory for others (Mandel 1962). With neo-liberal opening up of national economies, the 'unity and struggle' of transnational capital becomes a worldwide phenomenon. A significant portion of foreign investment in African countries goes into mergers and acquisitions. In an African periphery, monopoly capital is able to extract even greater concessions and super profits given the weakness of internal forces and the state. With opening up of their economies under neo-liberalism at the behest of the IFIs and imperial states, African economies have become more vulnerable as neo-liberal elites have assumed state power.

The configuration of internal classes and their alliance with foreign capital is evidently a concrete question requiring concrete investigation. Nonetheless, on a broad canvas, we may attempt some generalization at the level of SSA countries. The central question of political economy in SSA is agriculture or the producer on land. The locus of contradictions and the unfolding of the capitalist logic is the trilateral relationship between the state, the peasant, and capital. Two broad categories of countries may be identified: one where plantation agriculture dominates, the other where peasant agriculture is prevailing. The first case involved massive alienation of land to settlers under the hegemony of the colonial state (Kenya, Zimbabwe). The peasant producers were not fully proletarianised; rather they became a reservoir of cheap labour whether as squatters or as semi-proletarians on a reserve or on 'communal land.' Peasant labour thus subsidized settler capital. The land question was central to the struggle for national liberation. Formal independence from colonialism never fully resolved the land question. In post-independence Zimbabwe, the question remained *racialized* with the continued domination of white settlers. In Kenya, the mantle of the settler was taken over by the yeoman farmer or politicians and bureaucrats turned farmers, of a particular ethnic group, thus *ethnicizing* the land question. In both cases, it has exploded in violence. The land question is thus back on the historical agenda.

In the countries where peasant agriculture prevails, the debates have been on the *social* character of the peasantry and *modes* of exploitation of peasant labour. Nineteenth century writers on the agrarian question in Europe noted the continued existence of the peasant, the petty commodity producer, side by side with the development of capitalist agriculture. They argued that this was not because small production in agriculture was more viable or efficient, but rather because "small peasants reduce the level of their requirements below that of wage workers and tax their energies far more than the latter do ..." (Lenin 1966:27). However, they expected the peasant to disappear with further development of capitalist agriculture. It must be added, however, that Lenin's position had a political purpose. He was debunking the Narodniks who celebrated the small peasant (in modern discourse 'small is beautiful') and saw the peasant as the

69

harbinger of socialism, thus skipping or bypassing the capitalist stage. Neither the context nor the rationale of that debate applies to the continued existence of the African peasant. In our case, the peasant is not the remnant of the past, but integrated in the perverse capitalist logic of disarticulated accumulation.

I agree with Moyo and Yeros that there is no such thing as a peasant mode of production, nor does the peasant constitute a class. However, they over-simplify somewhat when they characterize the *whole* of the peasantry as semi-proletarian. The tendency for the differentiation of the peasantry into poor, middle, and rich peasant *a là* Mao does exist. This represents the so-called *American* path of the development of capitalist agriculture or accumulation from below, which is not the characteristic African agriculture. In the periphery the *American* path is blocked or distorted or perverted by the domination of various forms of *compradorial* capitals (merchant, state, petty bourgeois, etc.) which mediate between peasant labour and monopoly capital. To this must be added the disarticulation between agriculture and industry, the perverse nature of the latter being a major obstacle to 'accumulation from below'. The result is that agriculture is the site of generating, but not accumulating, surplus. It is accumulated *outside* agriculture, thereby reproducing stagnation and impoverishment in agriculture.

The intermediate *compradorial* capital may take different forms, including state or private, depending on the state of class struggles and the nature of global political economy, but its logic is grounded in accumulation by dispossession, that is, non-equivalent exchange. Financialisation of capitalism under neo-liberalism has spawned new forms of *compradorial* capitals, which exist in its interstices. This involves making quick money through expropriation of resources, which were hitherto in public domain or belonged to the commons such as birds and wildlife, timber, forest products, and biological resources. A new wave of enclosures is also in the making with the enclosing of beaches and mountains, waterfalls and streams, rare bio-species etc. for ecotourism. In this expropriation, the state as the ultimate custodian of public domain is closely involved. The political-bureaucratic class thus reaps political *rents* (corruption, bribes) by alienating the commons. They are *compradors* in the original Chinese sense of the word. The money thus obtained is not productively invested, but either expatriated to foreign banks or laundered in dubious financial institutions or speculative real estate markets. State positions, including its coercive powers, become the means of extracting surplus from producers, or expropriating values from weaker capitals. The enormous amount of money thus obtained is frittered away in conspicuous consumption by local elites, some of which borders on the absurd such as air freighting expensive motor vehicles for personal use, sending girlfriends to Paris for shopping, buying vacation bungalows in Dubai, or sending suits to London for dry-cleaning! Adebayo Adedeji describes this class well:

> A tiny group of actors in the unproductive and often illegal sector of the economy is setting the beat. They account for not more than 0.1 per cent of the population and are not only economically but also socially and culturally alienated from conditions in their countries. In fact, they are an international class[21], whose capital assets move swiftly in and out of countries around the globe. They ride on the restless wave of high-turnover financial capital. (Adedeji 1993: 7)

The short-term horizon of these entrepreneurs, or *wajisiriamali* as they are called in Tanzania, means that their 'investments' are geared to making quick profits such as entering into one-sided contracts, on utterly unequal terms, with the state or state companies (for example, Kiwira mines); using state positions or contacts to obtain lucrative tenders; colluding with dubious 'local and foreign investors' to establish front banks, exchange bureaus, or housing condominiums. It is amazing how massive skyscraper construction suddenly changes the skyline of cities in neo-liberalised economies from Thailand to Tanzania. Tearing down of old, but durable and, in some cases, beautiful buildings in the city centre of Dar es Salaam is an example of how speculative real estate markets work. It is driven by the supply of capital, rather than a demand (not *need*, of course) for housing. Of course, the consequence of pulling down buildings is to render occupants homeless, thus increasing the pool of unsheltered, who swell the numbers in ghettoes and slums. At the same time, apartments and offices in newly built, fully-furnished, concrete-and-glass blocks end up in the hands of a few wealthy speculators who buy them up and horde them with a view to rent or sell for higher gains. In the meantime, there are empty apartments waiting to be sold or rented existing side by side with a multitude of homeless. From the point of view of housing the seventy per cent of city inhabitants who 'live' in slum or unplanned areas, this real estate boom is irrational. It does not address the housing *need*; very often, it is not even demand-driven. The supply itself creates the demand and then the demand is speculative rather than need-based. Ironically, it is also unplanned because the existing infrastructure (water, electricity, roads, sewage, etc.) is simply dilapidated and inadequate to support high-rise buildings. The irrationality of such real estate development, from the point of view of social need, is epitomized by the recently announced multibillion dollar water front project on the seashores of the city of Dar es Salaam. Hundreds of square kilometers of the Indian Ocean will be reclaimed to create a new city centre of shopping malls and offices and presumably entertainment and gambling centres. In its own way, this form of real estate development also illustrates the disarticulated nature of accumulation in the periphery – disarticulation between the *need* and the *demand* for housing, and disarticulation between *demand* and *supply*.[22] Just as with other bubbles, the real estate bubble is built on quicksand; it is bound to collapse, as happened in Thailand during the Asian crash.

A disarticulated home market:

The development of the home market was integral to the development of capitalism in advanced countries. It is not surprising, therefore, that most of these countries adopted protective tariffs and related policies to fence off their home markets from external competition in the early period of their development. In extraverted economies, on the other hand, production is primarily for export. There is a decisive disjuncture between production and consumption in an export-enclave and import-substitution economies. The demand for the products of the primary productive sector (minerals, coffee, cotton, tea, etc) lies outside. There is no critical home market for these products. At the same time, the majority of the demand for the products of industry is the small elite, which means it comes from profits and rents rather than wages. The return to labour does not turn into a demand for the products of the modern sector, partly because they are expensive and partly because import substitution industries produce luxury goods, rather than goods for mass consumption. Wage goods come largely from the 'traditional' sector (food) or cheap imports like second hand clothing. Under neo-liberalism, the 'home market' is virtually destroyed as even staple foods like flour, oil, potatoes, tomatoes, vegetables, etc. are imported from outside by supermarket chains to the detriment of small domestic producers. The few local industries producing for mass consumption (textiles, leather, oil, soap etc.) go under with liberalization. Income distribution becomes skewed in favour of the small elites; salary bills rise in proportion to wage bills. The composition of imported consumer goods changes, catering for elite preferences, including the taste for gas-guzzling four-wheeled vehicles. Import bills rise; balance-of-payment problems ensue. IMF-type economists further advise increasing exportables by diversifying and exporting whatever is available, ostrich meat and eggs, cut flowers and game meat, precious stones and exotic timber. The ironic nature of the extraverted economy can be seen in 'middle-class' homes decorated with cheap plastic flowers imported from China, while fresh flowers are exported to Europe! De Janvry sums up the dilemma of the home market in peripheral capitalism thus: "The key difference between social articulation and disarticulation thus originates in the sphere of circulation – in the geographical and social location of the market for the modern sector. Under social articulation, market expansion originates principally in rising national wages; under disarticulation, it originates either abroad or in profits and rents" (De Janvry 1981: 34).

4

SUMMING UP: THE NATIONAL AND THE AGRARIAN QUESTIONS

The contradictory relationship between the African periphery and imperialism constitutes the *national question*. At the heart of this relationship lies the crisis of over-accumulation, which characterises capitalist imperialism. The *agrarian question* consists in the disarticulated accumulation that characterises peripheral capitalism. As we have seen, the two are linked inextricably in the worldwide process of capitalist expansion. In the immediate post-independence period, these questions were at the forefront of scholarly debates and political thought. The neo-liberal intervention entailed a paradigmatic shift. Grounded in the categories of the market and monetarism, neo-liberals had no way of problematising the processes of accumulation on the global or local level. The national and agrarian questions disappeared from the mainstream discourse. Among the leftist political economists, the debate simmered on, but there too there was a crisis with regard to the theory of *historical materialism,* particularly among the Western based leftist political economists. Some of the so-called internationalist Left, as Moyo and Yeros characterise them (2007a), argued that the national question either had been resolved or was no longer relevant. Meanwhile, the agrarian question had been resolved because the peasantry was fast disappearing. The peasant was no longer a pure agriculturalist; he/she was involved in multi-occupations and/ or thriving in the informal sector. What are essentially survival strategies, reinforcing the disarticulated forms of accumulation in response to the predatory financialisation of capitalism, are presented as a *progressive* dissolution of the peasant. Moyo and Yeros have succinctly discussed these debates in a number of their articles (2007a, 2007b, 2007c, 2007d). They take the position, with which we agree, that (a) the national and the agrarian questions remain unresolved; (b) they are inseparably linked and inserted in the global process of imperialist accumulation, which is characterised by (c) polarisation producing articulated accumulation at the centre and disarticulated accumulation at the periphery. Under disarticulated accumulation, capital shifts the burden of social reproduction to labour, thus neither the peasant nor the proletarian labour is fully proletarianised. Instead, the dominant tendency is for the semi-proletarianisation of labour in which the peasant or the worker (in the rural or urban area, in the formal or informal sectors) super-exploits himself/herself by cutting into his/her necessary consumption, a form of accumulation by dispossession.

On the transition to capitalism in agriculture, Lenin identified two paths of development, the *American* and the *Junker*. The American path refers to a situation in which accumulation by the peasantry results in its differentiation. This is accumulation from below. The Junker path is where landlords, or former feudal lords, turn capitalists, thus extracting surplus value from wage-labour as opposed to various forms of labour-rents from serfs.[23] In the former settler colonies such as Kenya and Zimbabwe, where there was massive alienation of land to settlers, agriculture development comes close to the Junker path except that it does not lead to a full scale development of capitalist agriculture, but rather exists as an enclave of super-exploitation and racial privilege under the overall domination of imperialist capital. Directly or indirectly, through the market or the state, settler agriculture is subsidised by semi-proletarian labour in the reserves and 'communal lands' or squatter labour on *latifundias*. The post-independence land resettlement program in Kenya, which was, in effect, a kind of market-based land reform, resulted in the Kenyanisation of settler farms. It did not change the fundamental relationship or the pattern of disarticulated accumulation in agriculture. Racial privileges were replaced by ethnic preferences that were underwritten by the neo-colonial state. In Zimbabwe, the Kenyan model did not take off, partly because of the intransigence of the former colonial state, Britain, and partly because of the deeper entrenchment of the settler class in the local political economy. In the plantation-settler African countries, the agrarian question is closely linked to the *land question*. Land reform has thus posed itself as a question of land redistribution. The immediate post-independence contestation was between the colonial/neo-colonial position advocating state-led, but market-based, land redistribution and a more nationalist position of radical 'expropriation of the expropriators'. The limits of the former can be seen in the Kenyan case. At the minimum, it can be said that the Kenyan model of 'land reform' fails to break the stranglehold of disarticulated accumulation and resolve the agrarian question. It does not fully unleash the *Junker* path of capitalist development in agriculture either; rather it assumes a new form of *compradorial* path. This is a further substantiation of the argument that the agrarian question cannot be resolved outside of, and separated from the national question. This brings us to the second, radical model of land reform – 'expropriation of the expropriators.' The vivid illustration of this 'model' is the land reform in Zimbabwe, which happened in the situation of crisis of the late 1990s and early 2000s in that country.

Moyo and Yeros (2007a, 2007b) are probably the only writers on the Left who have provided a consistent analysis of the Zimbabwe question rooted in the method of historical materialism and approached from the perspective of the national and agrarian questions. It is not necessary for our purpose to go into the details of their argument or position. More relevant is to pose the question: what would be the trajectory of accumulation *after* land redistribution and the creation of a small peasantry where the ultimate title and control of land is vested in the state? This question is not posed, much less answered, by the authors. This is so because there is considerable ambiguity in their analyses and position on the Zimbabwe question on the following issues: 1) Does the resolution of the land question also mean that the agrarian question is resolved? Land redistribution is necessary, but not sufficient for the resolution of the agrarian question. We have already argued that the agriculture revolution is not possible without industrialisation of agriculture, which in turn means the resolution of the national question to address the question of disarticulated accumulation. 2) The relation between the state, peasant, and land cannot be fully grasped without a clear analysis of the social character of the state and class and its relation with imperialism. To their credit, Moyo and Yeros, clearly recognise and emphasise that the transformation of peripheral capitalism is not simply a question of the structures of political economy, but fundamentally a political question of class struggle. Yet, they fudge over the class character of what they call the "radicalised state" in Zimbabwe. Their failure to differentiate between a *comprador* and a national bourgeoisie leads them

78

to identify the whole of black bourgeoisie, except for "a small section of the unaccommodated black bourgeoisie" (2007b:35) on the side of the pro-land reform nationalist bloc while at the same time, the working class (including farm labourers?) are part of the pro-imperialist "post-national alliance" (ibid.) The ambivalent attitude of the authors on these issues leads them unwittingly to fuse the national and race questions, thereby coming close to imply that the expropriation of land from white settlers and its occupation by black peasants has resolved the national question.

The characterisation and role of the local bourgeoisie in Africa, regardless of its racial and or ethnic composition,[24] and its relationship to imperialism has been quite problematic and the subject of heated debates on the African Left. Yet, class analysis of that kind is so essential to distinguish between the objective position of a class and its immediate political rhetoric on the one hand, and long-term tendencies of accumulation and conjuctural political factors, on the other. The peasant-state relationship and the land tenure system in some other SSA countries, where peasant production prevails, come close to the post-land reform situation in Zimbabwe.

A typical African social economy where peasant production prevails is characterised by:

a. Ultimate land ownership or control vests in the state governed by statutory law;

b. Immediate ownership is by family, clan, or village, governed by customary law;

c. Land is regulated by a hierarchical legal regime of customary and statutory law where statutory law prevails in case of conflict;[25]

d. Land sizes are small, *minifundia*;

e. The unit of production is a 'pure agriculturalist',[26] peasant household with a *functional* division between cash crops (mainly primary commodities for export) and food crop production, and a patriarchal division of labour between genders;

f. The household produces most of its subsistence while relying on the market for some critical items of consumption (salt, oil, clothing, etc) and inputs (chemicals, hoes etc.);

g. There is very little use of machinery, inorganic fertilisers, and irrigation in production; agriculture is largely rain-fed and labour-intensive; and

h. The typical source of energy is firewood.

The state stands in the position of a landlord in relation to the peasant producer. It may not directly extract ground rent, but does so indirectly through taxes, price differentials, adverse terms of trade, forced labour etc. Sovereignty and property merge in the state. The state's monopoly of violence, through law or otherwise (development conditions, minimum acreage laws, flat rate tax paid in cash, etc.) is exerted to keep the peasant chained to the capitalist system, although the process of peasant production itself is not capitalist. Extra economic coercion thus plays a central role in the process of peasant production.

Both land and labour productivity on peasant farms is low. While commodity production generates some differentiation within the peasantry, the process of accumulation is stuck at the level of rich peasant. For its further development and accumulation, the productivity has to rise. This can only happen by use of modern machinery and inorganic inputs, both of which are too expensive for the peasant and for the peripheral economy as a whole. Thus, surplus extracted from agriculture is not accumulated within agriculture to propel its industrialisation; rather it is accumulated as merchant capital to reproduce the extraverted economy. Merchant capital plays the role of intermediate capital between peasant labour and imperial capital. It can be private or state. Accumulation from below is thus blocked. It is merchantised, taking the path of 'accumulation from above', which is the characteristic feature of disarticulated accumulation.

Land reform in peasant economies presents itself as a land tenure reform. While the land question does not exist in the classical sense, it is not correct to say that in peasant economies it is only the agrarian question that needs to be addressed. Contestation over the type of land tenure reform represents different paths of development and trajectories of accumulation. The East African Royal Commission in the 1950s recommended individualisation, titling, and registration (ITR) as these countries approached independence. The argument was based on the alleged inefficiency of peasant production. Individualisation and titling would enable land to be used as collateral thus enabling investment in land. It would facilitate transfer of land from the inefficient to efficient farmers. It would penalise the lazy and the indolent while acting as an incentive to the hardworking. In Tanzania, Nyerere (1967) opposed the recommendation on the ground that if land became a commodity to be bought and sold like a shirt, it would create a class of landlords and another of the landless. It would be 'iffy' history to speculate on what would have happened had the recommendation been adopted. Fifty years later, the Peruvian neo-liberal Hernando de Costa came out with a new edition of the Royal Commission's argument under his thesis of formalising property,[27] which will be discussed fully in my forthcoming work.

Meanwhile, neighbouring Kenya did adopt the recommendations and embarked on the programme of consolidation and registration of land. The Commission's report came in the wake of the Mau Mau rebellion, which was centrally a struggle for land. In Kenya, the implementation of the Commission's recommendation was to create a yeoman farmer class, which would be the bulwark against radical change. It paved the way for the transition from colonialism to neo-colonialism, but failed to address the national and agrarian questions and put the country on a path of autocentric development. Instead, it ethnicised the land question. Fifty years later Kenya had its own land Commission that brought out the social inequities and the explosive nature of the land question. The post-election explosion in 2007-2008 resulting in the deaths of over 1000 people and bringing the country to the brink of collapse once again brought the land and the national questions back on the agenda, just as it is happening in many African countries in different forms.

Under neo-liberalism, predatory financial capital is heralding a new wave of commodification and expropriation of land. As predatory capital seeks over and underground natural resources, including massive amounts of land for agro-fuels, we can expect a new wave of expropriation of peasant lands and new forms

82

of accumulation by dispossession. In spite of the neo-liberal rhetoric, this process of primitive accumulation may not be disguised behind the invisible hand of the market. All indications are that the fist of the state backed by both the declining and the rising hegemonic powers will be deployed freely. The African peasantry is proving too resistant to the World Bank's pet project of ITR or De Sotto's mantra of formalising informal (customary) land tenure. The peasant wants the loans to develop his/her land but does not want it to be foreclosed on default. After 50 years of ITR in Kenya, the then President, Moi had to change the rules of foreclosure because bailiffs carrying court orders either faced peasants brandishing spears to defend their lands or did not know which lands to foreclose. The land registry in Nairobi did not reflect the real ownership situation on the ground where people continued to apply their customary laws in spite of having formally registered the land. So the path of commoditising land is proving to be too difficult. In practice, even the likes of the World Bank privately support forced alienations by the state to "capture" the peasant (Hyden's phrase) for the market while making ITR noises in public.

The land question is an intricate component of the agrarian question, which cannot be addressed without addressing the national question. At the end of the day, the real question is how to move from the disarticulated forms of accumulation to socially articulated forms. These questions cannot be answered in the abstract. They require a concrete analysis of the agency of change in the context of the state of international and national class struggles, which we hope to do in the ongoing study of the political economy of Tanzania.

AFTERWORD

As this manuscript was going to the press, the British Prime Minister Gordon Brown announced at the end of the G20 summit held in London at the beginning of April 2009 that the Washington consensus was over.

> The old Washington consensus is over. Today we have reached a new consensus that we take global action together to deal with the problems we face, that we will do what is necessary to restore growth and jobs, that we will take essential action to rebuild confidence and trust in our financial system and to prevent a crisis such as this ever happening again.[28]

One would have thought that Gordon Brown would have gone further and apologised on behalf of the G20's predecessor, the G7, for the social and economic havoc that the "Washington consensus" caused to millions of people, particularly in the South. One does not expect imperialist masters to apologise. The purpose of the G20 meeting was to revamp the capitalist-imperialist system in light of the crisis and changing balance of global power. One columnist characterised the G20 statement as essentially "an effort to rewrite the rules of capitalism", while Paul Taylor of Reuters opined that it was recognition of the shift in global power.

> The London G20 summit shows just how far power has ebbed from the United States, and from the West in general. Until late 2008, the Group of Eight mostly Western industrialized nations — the United States, Canada, Germany, France, Britain, Italy, Russia and Japan — was the key forum for economic governance.

> The new, unwieldy top table has emerged faster than anyone dared predict because a humbled America and a chastened Europe need the money and cooperation of rising powers such as China, India, Russia, Brazil and Saudi Arabia to fix the world economy.[29]

The top table is "unwieldy" because the former ghettoised countries from the global South - China, India, Brazil, and Saudi Arabia – are sharing it. Africa still has no place even at the "unwieldy" table. Instead, at the meeting of African finance ministers hosted by the IMF chief and President Kikwete of Tanzania in Dar es Salaam just weeks before the G20 summit, the IMF presented itself as the champion and spokesperson for Africa. In a public lecture at the University of Dar es Salaam, Dominique Strauss-Kahn said with a straight face that "The one policy suits all approach is wrong since countries have different needs. In one country privatization can be the solution while in another, the solution can be nationalisation."[30] All this was said with a straight face and without apology, when the IMF/World Bank-dictated privitisations have caused social upheavals and destruction of jobs and livelihoods in Africa. Virtually every major privitisation in Tanzania, for instance, from telecommunications to railways, banks and mines, has been a tragic tale of financial scandal and social upheaval.

This author subtitled his 2006 book *Let the People Speak* (Shivji 2006), "Tanzania down the road to neo-liberalism". We are now approaching the end of that road. It is time for the people to speak and for intellectuals to rethink, reassess, and chart out a new, alternative path for African development, a path that will never again marginalise African masses under the spurious rule of elites in collusion with imperialism.

Together with the approaching end of neo-liberalism, the development discourse will also need to change. 'Poverty reduction or alleviation' strategies, which dismissed the masses as the poor, while elevating the so-called private sector (meaning private capital) as the 'engine of growth', need to be subjected to close scrutiny. The scrutiny has begun. As Gordon Brown was burying the "Washington consensus" in London, Thandika Mkandawire, a respected African scholar, was addressing REPOA researchers in Dar es Salaam on "the role of the state for market-led development in a developing economy". While reaffirming the role of a developmental state in Africa, Mkandawire pointedly questioned the meaning of "market-led development". Markets do not lead; it is social actors who lead, he asserted. The central question, therefore, is which social actors and what type of state would lead development in Africa. In other words, we need to discover – concretely – the agency of development.

The questions raised in the last section of this monograph are therefore very pertinent. We need to go back to the basics of political economy. The national, social, and agrarian questions need to be addressed, analysed, and understood so as to discover the agency for social change and transformation in Africa. This time around we need to go further and revisit the vision of pan-Africanism. The last fifty years of African independence have proved the futility of pursuing "narrow territorial nationalisms". The pursuit of development at the level of *vinchi* (state-lets), as Nyerere used to call African countries, has brought little development and much less democracy. Just as development is back on the historical agenda, so is pan-Africanism. The first three volumes of Nyerere's speeches were titled *Freedom and Unity, Freedom and Socialism,* and *Freedom and Development.*

Had he lived, the fourth volume may well have been titled *Freedom and Pan-Africanism.*

Dar es Salaam
5 April 2009

REFERENCES

Adedeji, A., ed. 1993, *Africa within the World: Beyond Dispossession and Dependence*, London: Zed books.

Adedeji, A., 1993, "Marginalisation and Marginality", in Adedeji ed. op.cit: 1-14.

Adesina, J. O. et al. eds., 2006, *Africa & Development: Challenges in the New Millennium*, Dakar, London & Pretoria: CODESRIA, Zed & UNISA Press.

Amara, Hamid Ait & B. F. Tchuigoua eds. 1990, *African Agriculture: The Critical Choices*, London: Zed.

Amin, S. 1990a, *Maldevelopment: Anatomy of a Global Failure,* London: Zed.

Amin, S., 1990b, "The Agricultural Revolution and Industrialization," in Amara & Tchuigoua eds. op. cit:1-11.

Amsden, H. Alice, 2001, *The Rise of "the Rest": Challenges to the West from Late-Industrialization Economies*, Oxford University Press.

Anyemedu, K., 2006, "Financing Africa's Development: Can Aid Dependence be Avoided?", in Adesina ed. op. cit: 256-274.

Baran, P., 1957, *The Political Economy of Growth,* New York: MR Press.

Baran, P. and P. Sweezy, 1966, *Monopoly Capital*, New York: Monthly Review Press.

BBC, 2001, "World inequality rises", 18/07/2001, at http://news.bbc.co.uk/2/hi/ buisness/1442073. Item accessed on 30/03/2008.

Bello, Walden, 2008, "Capitalism in an Apocalyptic Mood," *Focus on Trade*, Number 137, February 2008, A Weekly Online Magazine.

Bowles, S., et al. eds. 2005, *Understanding Capitalism,* Oxford: Oxford University Press.

Blair's Commission for Africa. *Commission for Africa, Our Common Interest,*

Report of the Commission for Africa Executive Summary at http://www.commissionforafrica.org/english/report/thereport/english/11-03-05_cr_executive_summary.pdf

Brandt Commission, 1980, *North-South: A Programme for Survival,* MIT Press.

Cabral, A., 1980, *Unity and Struggle: Speeches and Writings,* London: Heinemann.

Cooper, Robert, 2002, "The Post-Modern State", in Mark Leonard ed. *Re-ordering the World: The long-term implications of September 11th,* a Foreign Policy Centre Publication. The article is accessible at http://fpc.org.uk/article/169 accessed on 29.03.2008.

Fanon, F., 1963, *The Wretched of the Earth*, London: Penguin.

Furedi, F., 1994, *The New Ideology of Imperialism,* London: Pluto.

Davidson, B., 1971 [1963] *Black Mother: A Study of the Precolonial connection between Africa and Europe,* London: Longman.

De Janvry, A. 1981, *The Agrarian Question and Reformism in Latin America*, Baltimore: John Hopkins.

Development Dialogue, 2006, *Carbon Trading: a critical conversation on climate change, privatisation and power,* no. 48, September 2006.

Galeano, E., 1971, *Open Veins of Latin America: Five Centuries of the Pillage of a Continent*, New York: MR Press.

Gibbon, P., 1995, "Merchantisation of Production and Privatisation of Development in Post-*Ujamaa* Tanzania: An Introduction", in Peter Gibbon, ed. 1995. *Liberalised Development in Tanzania: Studies on Accumulation Processes and Local Institutions*, Uppsala: Nordiska Afrikainstututet op. cit. 9-36.

Harvey, D., 2003, *The New Imperialism*, Oxford: Oxford University Press.

Harvey, D., 2005, *A Brief History of Neoliberalism*, Oxford: Oxford University Press.

Hettne, B., 1990, *Development Theory and the Three Worlds,* London: Longman.

Hyden, G., 1980, *Beyond Ujamaa in Tanzania: Underdevelopment and an Uncaptured Peasantry,* Berkely & Los Angeles: University of California Press.

Iliffe, J., ed. 1973, *Modern Tanzanians: A Volume of Biographies*, Nairobi: East African Publishing House.

Irvin, G., 2007, "Growing Inequality in the Neo-liberal Heartland," *post-autistic economic review,* issue no. 43.

Jha, P. Shanker, 2006, *The Twilight of the Nation State: Globalisation, Chaos and War*, New Delhi: Vistaar.

Khanna, P., 2008, "Waving Goodbye to Hegemony", *New York Times*, January 27, 2008. at http://www.nytimes. com/2008/01/27/magazine/27world-t.html? r=2&ei=5070&en=4be... Accessed 3/3/2008.

Kjekshus, H., 1977, *Ecology Control and Economic Development in East African History: The Case of Tanganyika 1850-*

1950, London: Heinemann.

Korten, D. C., 1996, *When Corporations Rule the World*, Connecticut: Kumarian Press.

Kuuya, M., 1980, "Import Substitution as an Industrial Strategy: The Tanzanian Case", in Rweyemamu ed. Op. cit:69-91.

LeMelle, G., 2008, "Africa Policy Outlook 2008," *Foreign Policy in Focus*, www.fpif.org.

Lenin, V. I., [1917] 1966, *Imperialism: The Highest Stage of Capitalism,* Moscow: Progress Publishers.

Loong, Yin Shao, 2007, "Debt: The Repudiation Option", *Third World Resurgence* Nos.198-199, Feb./March 2007.

Luxembourg, R., [1913] 1963, *The Accumulation of Capital*, London: Routledge.

Luxembourg, R., & N. Bukharin, [1915, 1924] 1972, *Imperialism and the Accumulation of Capital,* London: Penguin.

Magdoff, H., 1969, *The Age of Imperialism: The Economics of US Foreign Policy*, New York: MR Press.

Mamdani, M. 2004, *Good Muslim, Bad Muslim: America, the Cold War, and the Roots of Terror,* New York: Pantheon Books.

Mandel, E., 1962, 1968, *Marxist Economic Theory*, London: Merlin.

Marx, K, 1867, *Capital*, Vol. I, Moscow: Progress Publishers.

Marx, K. [1859] 1971, *A Contribution to the Critique of Political Economy*, London: Lawrence & Wishart.

Mboya, T., 1963, *Freedom and After*, London: Andre Deutsch.

Milanovic, B., 2007, "An even higher global inequality than previously thought: a note on global inequality calculations based using the 2005 ICP results", preliminary draft at http://siteresources.worldbank. org/INTDECINEQ/Resources/GlobalInequality. pdf accessed on 4/04/2009.Mkandawire, T. & C. C. Soludo, eds., 1999, *Our Continent, Our Future: African perspectives on structural adjustment*, Dakar: CODESRIA.

Mkandawire, T., 2001, "Thinking about developmental states in Africa", *Cambridge Journal of Economics*, 25: 289-315.

Moyo, S. and Paris Yeros, eds., 2007(a), *Reclaiming the Land: The Resurgence of Rural Movements in Africa, Asia and Latin America*, London & Cape Town: Zed Books and David Philip.

Moyo, S. and Paris Yeros, 2007(b), "The Resurgence of Rural Movements under Neoliberalism", in Moyo and Yeros, eds., *The Resurgence*, op. cit. pp.8-64.

Moyo, S. and Paris Yeros, 2007(c), "The Zimbabwe Question and the Two Lefts", in *Historical Materialism*, 15,4:

Moyo, S. and Paris Yeros, 2007(d), "The Radicalised State: Zimbabwe's Interrupted Revolution", *Review of African Political Economy*, 111: 103-121.

Neocosmas, M., 1993, *The Agrarian Question in Southern Africa and "Accumulation from Below"*, Uppsala: The Scandinavian Institute for African Studies.

Nkrumah, K. 1965, *Neo-Colonialism: the Last Stage of Imperialism*, London: Heinemann.

Nyerere, J. K., 1958, "National Property" in Nyerere 1967 op. cit.: pp. 53-58

Nyerere, J. K., 1967, *Freedom and Unity: a selection from writings and speeches*, Dar es Salaam: Oxford University Press.

Onimode, B., 1993, "The Imperatives of Self-Confidence and Self-Reliance in African Development", in Adedeji ed. op. cit:184-196.

Owen, R. and Bob Sutcliffe, eds. 1972, *Studies in the Theory of Imperialism*, London: Longman.

Peacock, A. 2002, *Two Hundred Pharaohs Five Billion Slaves*, London: Ellipsis.

Rasheed, S., 1993, "Africa at the Doorstep of the Twenty-First Century: Can Crisis Turn into Opportunity," in Adedeji ed. op. cit: 41-58.

Rodney, W. 1972, *How Europe Underdeveloped Africa*, Dar es Salaam: Tanzania Publishing House.

Ruhumbika ed. 1974, *Towards Ujamaa: twenty years of Tanu leadership*, Nairobi: East African Literature Bureau.

Rweyemamu, J., 1973, *Underdevelopment and Industrialization in Tanzania*, Oxford: Oxford University Press.

Rweyemamu, J., ed. 1980, *Industrialization and Income Distribution in Africa,* Dakar: CODESRIA.

Rweyemamu, J., 1980, "Introduction: Agenda for Research", in Rweyemamu ed. op.cit:1-13.

Sangare, S., 2003, "Industrialisation in Africa: A New Approach", in Adesina ed. op. cit: 140-151.

Saul, J. & Lionel Cliffe, 1972, *Socialism in Tanzania: An Interdisciplinary Reader*, Nairobi: East African publishing House.

Shivji, I. G., 1986 (a), *Law, State and the Working Class in Tanzania*, London: James Currey.

Shivji, I. G., ed. 1986 (b), *The State and the Working People in Tanzania*, Dakar: CODESRIA.

Shivji, I. G., 1987, "The Roots of Agrarian Crisis in Tanzania- A

Theoretical Perspective" in *Eastern Africa Social Science Research Review* III, 1:111-134.

Shivji, I. G., 1993, *Intellectuals at the Hill: Essays and Talks 1969-1993*, Dar es Salaam: DUP.

Shivji, I. G., 2002, "Globalisation and Popular Resistance", in Semboja, J. et al. *Local Perspectives on Globalisation: The African Case,* Dar es Salaam: REPOA.

Shivji, I. G., 2003, "Three Generations of Constitutions and Constitution-making in Africa: An Overview and Assessment in Social and Economic Context" in Mihaela Şerban Rosen ed. *Constitutionalism in Transition: Africa and Eastern Europe*, Warsaw: Helsinki Foundation for Human Rights, pp. 74-92.

Shivji, I.G. 2005, "The Rise, the Fall and the Insurrection of Nationalism in Africa", in Felicia Arudo Yieke ed. *East Africa: In Search of National and Regional Renewal,* Dakar: CODESRIA.

Shivji, I. G., 2006, *Let the People Speak: Tanzania down the road to neo-liberalism*, Dakar: CODESRIA.

Silverstein, K., 1997, "Privatizing War: How Affairs of State are Outsourced to Corporations Beyond Public Control," *The Nation*, July 28/August 4, 1997.

South Commission, the, 1990, *The Challenge to the South: The Report of the South Commission,* London: Oxford University Press.

Stiglitz, J., 2002, *Globalization and its Discontents*, New York: Norton.

Tan, Celine, 2008, "Zambian debt case highlights new threat to debt-relief countries", *Third World Resurgence, No.*198/199.

Tandon, Y., 1982, *University of Dar es Salaam: debate on class, state & imperialism,* Dar es Salaam: Tanzania Publishing House.

TANU, 1967, *Arusha Declaration*, Dar es Salaam: Government Printer.

Third World Network, 2003, "Cancun 1, Cancun II, and trying to repeat rewritten history?", at http://www.twnside. org.sg/title/5430a.html, accessed 2/6/2008.

Third World Resurgence, 2007, "Biofuels: An illusion and a threat", No. 200, April 2007: pp.6-26.

Toussaint, E. 1999, *Your Money or Your Life! the tyranny of global finance,* London: Pluto Press.

US Embassy. 29 July, 2003, Press Release Dar es Salaam.

Warren, B., 1982, *Imperialism: Pioneer of Capitalism*, London: NLB-Verso.

Williams, Eric, 1964, *Capitalism and Slavery*, London: Andre Deutch.

Wood, E. M., 2003, *Empire of Capital*, London: Verso.

World Bank, 1981, *Accelerated Development in Sub-Saharan Africa: An Agenda for Africa.* World Bank.

.

Endnotes

1. Ironically, Africa loses an estimated 200,000 experts through 'brain drain', while it receives some 80,000 so-called experts from the North to implement its technical programmes (Onimode 1993: 191).

2. The irony of Blair's Africa Commission turns cynical when it is recalled that one of Blair's commissioners, President Mkapa, comes from the same country, whose first President, Nyerere, in retirement, chaired the South Commission which was conceived and financed by the South!

3. Page numbers are from the hardcover edition published by Progress Publishers, Moscow, which is not dated.

4. So-called because of their adherence to neo-liberal theories taught by Friedman at the University of Chicago.

5. Both Friedman and Hayek were the supporters of the Chilean dictator Pinochet. In answer to a journalist regarding Pinochet's dictatorship in 1981, Hayek said: "A dictator may rule in a liberal way, just as it [is] possible for a democracy to rule without the slightest liberalism. My personal preference is for a liberal dictatorship rather than a democratic government thoroughly lacking in liberalism" (Quoted in Toussaint 1999:182).

6. Warren (1982) used this argument to develop his controversial thesis on "imperialism as a pioneer of capitalism" and therefore as progressive in the 1970s.

7   For the debates of the 1970s on imperialism, see Owen and Sutcliffe 1972.

8   For some interesting insights, see Wood (2003: 130 et. Seq.)

9   For a useful account of militarism in the US foreign policy since 9/11, see Mamdani 2004.

10 During the early phase of the introduction of neo-liberalism, the then Tanzanian Minister of Finance was reported to have made this famous remark on the floor of the Parliament: *kila mtu abebe msalaba wake* (Let everyone carry his/her cross.).

11 Since leaving office, Blair has become the Quartet's Special Envoy in the Middle East "peace talks"; advises an insurance company on the risks of climate change, a bank on crisis management, and Rwanda on good governance, all of which, except that with Rwanda, are paid jobs. He has also taken up a teaching assignment at Bush's alma mater, Yale, where he will teach a course on faith and globalisation in the schools of management and divinity. Finally he is about to launch his Faith Foundation. There could not be a better combination of the characteristics of a neo-liberal in one man! (See *The African on Sunday*, March 9, 2008).

12 Marx takes the words in double-quotation marks from his preliminary work on political economy published seven years before *Capital* called *A Contribution to the Critique of Political Economy* (1971: 27 [1859]).

13 The trend began earlier under Clinton and has developed to frightening proportions since then (See Silverstein 1997).

14 For example, USAID is projected to work closely with the

Department of Defence under AFRICOM (Lemelle 2008:5).

15 The new labour laws passed by Tanzania, with the aid of a South African consultant funded by Denmark and pushed by Mkapa in a hothouse fashion, are premised on contractual, as opposed to permanent, employment.

16 A case in point is the recent example in Tanzania where the pressure exerted by the Confederation of Industries of Tanzania (CIT), which, strictly, is not even an employers' organization, forced the government to change unilaterally the minimum wage recommended by the tripartite wage boards.

17 Some $133 million thus disappeared from the External Payment Arrears (EPA) account of the Bank of Tanzania in 2008.

18 In principle, I do not see a fundamental difference between "cash transfers" to alleviate poverty and individual charity to alleviate the plight of a beggar. In the latter case, at least, there is a veneer of altruism; the former is a straight foreign-policy tool for the donor government, and another opportunity for private accumulation for the receiving-government's bureaucrats.

19 For example, when Tanzania decided to establish a cement plant in 1964, it could have been located in any of the four potential areas – Dar es Salaam, Kilwa, Tanga, or Mbeya. For the long-term development of the country, Kilwa was most suited because it has vast gypsum deposits. The plant could have produced sulphuric acid, which is one of the most used acids in industry. The chemical process of making cement from gypsum requires coke. Thus, coal deposits in the south

of the country could have been exploited to provide fuel. This could have been linked to the exploitation of iron ore also in the south. Instead, in the interest of foreign shareholders, the plant was located 25 kilometers from Dar es Salaam, using imported oil for fuel and electricity for energy (Kuuya 1980: 79-82).

[20] They are street hawkers, between 16 to 25 years of age, fresh from the countryside. They walk anything between 15 to 25 kilometers a day; drink water for their lunch or sniff a hard substance to kill appetite; live in single rooms in Swahili houses; in some cases doubling up as pimps and providers of sexual pleasures to their landladies in lieu of rent; exploit every opportunity during the day to steal and mug while hawking; suppress their pains and injuries with heavy doses of *panadols* and *cafenols* and eventually end up in some city mortuary buried by the municipality for lack of next of kin. Is this the kind of multi-occupational diversification of the informal sector that researchers celebrate?

[21] This is slightly exaggerated, although the sentiment is correct. The neo-liberal African elites are more a caricature of their international counterparts, rather than a part of the international elite.

[22] The housing boom has pushed up the cement prices between 70 to 100 per cent in Tanzania within the last 4-5 years. Real estate construction is not affected because contractors pass on the increase to their clients who in turn pass it on to their customers. Public works (roads, bridges, schools) and lower middle class homebuilders suffer. Thus the sufferers are not

real estate developers, whose demand was responsible for the price rise in the first place, but the wider public. So much for rational allocation of resources by the invisible hand of the market! Mkapa's demagogic minister for lands visibly deployed the fist of the state in favour of dubious real estate developers. They went so far as to create an artificial demand for housing by the government for public servants after selling off government houses to their occupants at fire-sale prices.

23 For a succinct summary of Lenin's position, see Neocosmas (1993).

24 This is not to say that the ethnic/racial character of exploiter and exploited classes are not important, particularly when elites use these to justify their enrichment or get into political power. But one must not confuse forms of consciousness with categories of analysis.

25 In legal circles the continued existence of customary law side by side with statutory law is wrongly called legal pluralism.

26 Colonialism destroyed the incipient domestic manufactory and craft industry, that is, the beginnings of division between agriculture and manufacturing (Kjekshus 1977).

27 This is the basis of the so-called programme for formalising property ('*mkurabita*').

28 http://www.pressrun.net/weblog/2009/04/old-washington-consensus-is-over-gordon-brown.html accessed on 4/04/2009

29 Ibid.

30 The Citizen, Tanzania, 10/03/2009.